POWER EVANGELISM
JUST DO IT!

POWER EVANGELISM
JUST DO IT!

MATTHEW HELLAND

ARROWZ

Power Evangelism—Just Do It

Copyright © 2020 Matthew Helland

Published by Arrowz Publishing House
info@arrowz.org
www.arrowz.org

Author: Matthew Helland
Editor: Erica Kramer
Art direction and interior design: Ronald Gabrielsen, 3ig.org

ISBN 978 1 951014 06 3 (Powerpocket)
ISBN 978 1 951014 07 0 (eBook)

The Gray Matrix © Frank Gray, thegraymatrix.org. Used by permission.
The graphic by Putty Putman, © Putty Putman. Used by permission.
Prayers in chapter 3, © Neil Cole. Used by permission.

Unless otherwise noted, all Scripture quotations are from the ESV® Bible (The Holy Bible, English Standard Version®), copyright © 2001 by Crossway, a publishing ministry of Good News Publishers. Used by permission. All rights reserved.

Scriptures marked (NLT) are taken from the HOLY BIBLE, NEW LIVING TRANSLATION, Copyright © 1996, 2004, 2007 by Tyndale House Foundation. Used by permission of Tyndale House Publishers, Inc., Carol Stream, Illinois 60188. All rights reserved. Used by permission.

Any italics in Bible passages have been added by the author.

All rights reserved. No portion of this book may be reproduced, stored in a retrieval system or transmitted in any form, electronically, mechanically, by means of photocopying, recording or otherwise—with the exception of brief quotation in printed reviews—without the prior written permission of the publisher.

I dedicate this book to my four children.

*My life's greatest honor and delight
is being your papa.
You make me happy, proud and satisfied.
My prayer is that you will always
hear my voice and the voice of God
resounding in your heart saying,*

*"You are my beloved child.
I am proud of you.
I love you!"*

*And proclaim as you go, saying,
'The kingdom of heaven is at hand.'
Heal the sick, raise the dead,
cleanse lepers, cast out demons.
You received without paying;
give without pay.*
– Matthew 10:7-8

Contents

Endorsements	9
Foreword	13
Introduction: Love and Power	15
1. The Power of Love	23
2. The Gospel of Love	39
3. How People Come to Christ	53
4. Intimacy and Authority	75
5. How to Heal the Sick	87
6. How to Use Words of Knowledge	103
7. How to Grow in Power Evangelism	119
Conclusion: Just Do "The Stuff"	139
Notes	146
Recommended Resources	148
About the Author	151

Cutting-Edge Materials
for Radical Followers of Jesus

Visit us at
arrowz.us

For questions and bulk discount orders
please contact us at info@arrowz.us

Endorsements

I have known Matthew for more than thirty years, and he is the real deal. He was in love with Jesus as a young man and I have watched the passion and commitment grow. In this book, Matt is unpacking one of his favorite subjects, "How to do the Jesus stuff." He invites you and me into the great adventure of following the nudges of the Holy Spirit, engaging the world with the words and works of Jesus. Enjoy!

– *Phil Strout*
National Director, Vineyard USA

I strongly encourage every follower of Jesus to study this book. I was inspired in my faith and walk with Christ, and I know you will be too.

– *Dr Doug Beacham*
Bishop, International Pentecostal Holiness Church

Matthew Helland is a bold, loving practitioner of the gospel of the Kingdom. He does what he teaches and equips others in: prophecy, healing, deliverance and power evangelism. *Power*

Evangelism—Just Do It is an accessible manual that will ground you in the heart of God and empower you with the tools necessary to demonstrate and proclaim the Kingdom. Read it, and jump in on the fun!

– *Putty Putman*
Author, speaker, initiator School of Kingdom Ministry

Power Evangelism—Just Do It! is a fantastic book that will encourage you to get going, because every Christian can bring the Gospel with God's love and His supernatural power.

– *Herman Boon*
Leader, Prayer & Fasting Conferences in the Netherlands

Matthew Helland uses the gifts of the Holy Spirit to reach lost and hurting people and he can teach you to do the same. His stories from the frontlines of real-life evangelism will inspire you to tap into the power of the Holy Spirit so you can share your faith with boldness and confidence. From the Red-Light District of Amsterdam to the heart of South America, Matthew Helland has proven the principles of power evangelism work in a modern age. If you want to be used by God to do amazing things, read this book!

– *Dr. Daniel King*
Missionary, evangelist, humanitarian

This beautiful book by Matthew Helland teaches us to evangelize. Matt invites us to do that the way Jesus did it: with love and power, using prophecy, healing and deliverance, and by being aware of God's presence.

Being Dutch Reformed, in the past, I wouldn't have embraced this type of evangelism. That has changed, because I have seen the results when we allow God to be in charge and are willing to listen to His voice and pray for people.

– *Hans Maat*
Director, Evangelisch Werkverband
binnen de Protestantse Kerk van Nederland

This book is a complete power evangelism manual, now it's up to you to "Just Do It."

– *Roger Cunningham Sr*
Pastor, La Viña de Las Condes, Santiago, Chile

This is an awesome book, a must-read for every pastor and every Christian with a heart to share the Gospel in a relevant and meaningful way. Matthew shares real-life, hands-on experiences with power evangelism. This is a real eye-opener for many of us. God still works in miraculous ways. This book is a beautiful invitation to cooperate with the Holy Spirit in reaching out to a world desperately in need of a loving God.

– *Bram Vlasblom*
Pastor, Vineyard Church, Utrecht, the Netherlands

Foreword

Power Evangelism—Just Do It! by Matthew Helland is an important book for this generation.

My first encounter with power evangelism was in 1985, when I was a new, young believer. I walked into a church in Anaheim, California to hear a man named John Wimber preach. A few years later, while I was a student at a Baptist college, I purchased his book *Power Evangelism*. The book has had a great impact on my life and for the past thirty years, power evangelism has been part of my ministry. The fruit is 1.1 million names added to the Lamb's Book of Life.

Not long ago, I met Matthew Helland on a ministry trip to Chile. The way he lived and loved caught my attention. I watched as he prioritized love as the goal of discipleship. Matthew spent most of his time empowering the ordinary people around him to do extraordinary things for Jesus. As a result, the supernatural looked very natural.

Power Evangelism—Just Do It! is a must-read for anyone who wants to bring glory to Jesus by living and loving just the way He does. Matthew is a reliable guide who can train and equip you in Jesus' Kingdom ministry. You can trust this guidebook:

it is biblical, practical, personal and simple! The pages are full of revelation, impartation and activation.

However, I must warn you: If you read the book and let the book read you, your life can make it hard for people to go to hell and easy for people to go to heaven!

– *Leif Hetland*

President of Global Mission Awareness
Author of "Called to Reign" and "Giant Slayers"

INTRODUCTION
Love and Power

An ordinary day in Amsterdam's Red-Light District. Women sit behind windows, lit by fluorescent red lights. The streets are teeming with customers and sightseers.

Behind one of the windows, a woman we will call Laura sees a guy approach her. Is he a potential client?

No, there is a woman with him, a Christian who visits her every week. "It's just those Christians coming to talk to me," she thinks. As they come into her workplace, greetings are exchanged.

The man introduces himself as Frits Rouvoet, the woman's father.

"So, how have you been?" they ask her.

Laura says, "Well, my back and knees really hurt. I've been weeding a garden."

Rouvoet says, "That's right. I see a picture of you kneeling, trying to help someone."

Laura responds, "I always want to help people, but I can't even help myself."

But she also thinks, "What's that about this guy seeing me on my knees in a picture? That's awkward! I hope he doesn't tell me I have to become a Christian. There is *no way* I am becoming a Christian."

Rouvoet asks, "Is it okay if I pray for you?"

"Sure."

Rouvoet prays a very simple prayer: "Father God, I ask you to take Laura to a very safe place. Let her sit on Your lap and feel Your embrace and love."

Laura feels her knees buckle and she falls to the ground. She sees an amazing vision: angels in khaki pants coming toward her. They carry water from a clean fountain and have towels. They wash her completely. As she starts to get up, all pain in her body is gone and God speaks to her, saying, "What do you want to do? Do want to accept Jesus? Do you want to follow Me?"

She does not immediately respond, but when she tells Rouvoet what just happened, she says, "I want to accept Jesus."

When she talks to her colleagues later that day, they ask her who she is in love with. Her face is beaming with joy.

She simply answers, "I have met Jesus and I will never be the same again."

Laura goes home and tells her mother, "I am getting out of prostitution right now!"

The first thing her mom says is, "Honey, are you high?" But Laura is not on drugs, she has had a power encounter with Jesus Christ. And it started with Rouvoet sharing God's love and power. Rouvoet's ministry Bright Fame has helped Laura and several of her colleagues get out of prostitution. Both Laura and her mother are now members of our local church.

My wife, Femke, and I have the honor of serving as pastors with Bright Fame and Scharlaken Koord among people working in Amsterdam's Red-Light District. On a regular basis, the people we pray with experience God's presence and healing. Their hearts are touched by prophecy and words of knowledge. Lives are transformed! All because of power evangelism.

What is Power Evangelism?

The term "power evangelism" was first made popular by the late John Wimber in his book that carried that title.[1] Power evangelism is using prophecy, healing, deliverance and the presence of God to share the Gospel.[2] It is especially effective in a culture that focuses on rational arguments for or against God: it bypasses people's minds and touches their hearts or bodies with God's power. People who experience God's love and power are generally much more open to hearing about Jesus. For believers, too, power evangelism has benefits. It strengthens our faith and opens up all channels to God and to the Church.

Power evangelism is not the sole domain of extraverts. It isn't just meant for street evangelism. It is simply sharing God's good news. It is making God's presence tangible, not just sharing his truths, but demonstrating His power. If you can share God's love with people and pray for someone, power evangelism is for you. It is for every believer and for everyday life. Every believer can pray for the sick and every believer can get a word from God (Mark 16:15-18; Jer. 33:3).

There is a biblical mandate for power evangelism. Jesus Himself released God's power in signs and wonders, and He says, "Truly, truly, I say to you, whoever believes in me will also do the works that I do; and greater works than these will he do, because I am going to the Father" (John 14:12). The same Holy Spirit who raised Jesus from the dead is now at work in us (see Rom. 8:10-11). He calls us to "heal the sick, raise the dead, cleanse lepers, cast out demons" and freely give what has been given to us (Matt. 10:7-8). In other words, signs and wonders are supposed to follow the preaching of His Word so that people know that He is real. Jesus Christ is our best example of a power evangelist.

The apostle Paul followed in Jesus' footsteps. His primary evangelism and church-planting strategy was to go into an area and let the Holy Spirit use him to change lives by means of signs and wonders. He healed the sick, raised the dead, prophesied, and got words of knowledge throughout his missionary journeys (see Acts 20:7-12; 27:22-26; 28:8-9). He was continually doing Holy Spirit signs and wonders everywhere he went (Rom. 15:18-20).

Paul preached the Gospel from Jerusalem to Illyricum, traveling by boat and road. Nowadays, we have modern air travel, so we can share the Gospel even more widely using the same ministry methods. In fact, even the flights themselves can be used for evangelistic purposes!

As I was flying to a Middle-Eastern nation to teach on power evangelism, I happened to sit next to a pastor from a traditional church. I told him that I train people in evangelism using healing, prophecy and words of knowledge. I explained that when I meet people, I ask them if they have pain in their body or if I can share what I see in them before I begin talking about Jesus. He looked at me and said, "Why do you do that?" For him and many other believers, power evangelism is something foreign and not for today.

On the flight back, a woman sitting next to me seemed puzzled when I told her that I was a pastor of a church. For her, pastors were old men dressed up in dusty robes leading people in a ceremony.

I asked her, "Is your back hurting?"

Her jaw dropped. "Yes," she answered.

And so I prayed for her. All pain disappeared. For the next hour of the flight, I was able to explain the Gospel and pray with her. The next time I preached in her city, she brought along a friend. They walked up to me, and she introduced me as: "The pastor I met on the airplane, who did not care about people's background, but really wanted people to get to know God. He loves people just as they are."

Love and Power

When we share Jesus' message, we should do it the way He did: with love and power. Everything He did was based on love. Jesus became friends with sinners and outcasts and had dinner with them. And God's power was at the heart of Jesus' ministry. Jesus used healing, words of knowledge, prophecy and deliverance to transform people's lives.

What Jesus did two thousand years ago, He also wants to do today through normal believers like you and me. He wants us to share His love and power with others. If you take either love or power out of the equation when you evangelize, you end up with less than God's best.

Without love, evangelism becomes insensitive and bullish; the message shared lacks God's heart. It cannot properly be called 'the Gospel'; after all, it isn't really good news. I have witnessed people who operate in God's power without understanding the Gospel. Their spiritual gifts of prophecy or healing are legitimate, but they use them in a destructive manner. Effective power evangelism can only happen when the evangelist shares from the overflow of their relationship with God.

But evangelizing without power has also proven ineffective. Many Western Christians have embraced a rational form of Christianity that is devoid of any supernatural power. If believers need healing, they will generally just take an aspirin and not even consider praying for it. How will non-believers get to know Jesus if they do not realize He is alive and active and ready to intervene in their lives? I love to hear the testimonies of people in my church who have been healed and set free from addiction, depression and issues which seemed impossible to change. With God there is nothing impossible or too difficult. If Jesus' love and power flows through us, however, we have very good news for people. If we allow the Gospel to shape the core of our being, evangelism will flow out of who God is in us. Knowing Christ and allowing His message to reach the deepest part of our being changes us from the inside out. This is why I titled this book *Power Evangelism—Just Do It!* Evangelism shouldn't be another activity on our to-do list, but a natural outflow of who we are.

Most books about evangelism focus on wisdom and good arguments to believe in God. This book will focus on doing what Jesus said we can do in the power of the Holy Spirit. I will explain how the Gospel is radically different from self-righteous, legalistic religion. I will write about the process of evangelism, the motivation for evangelism and lay down a biblical foundation for power evangelism. I will explain how you can grow in power evangelism.

I once dreamed I was loading a ship with gunpowder and dynamite. I knew this dream was a parable about equipping people with the Holy Spirit's power gifts. Dynamite and gunpowder are great tools if you are going to build roads through mountains, but deadly if you use them to blow up people. Prophecy, words of knowledge, healing and deliverance are powerful tools that can deliver great results, but if they are misused, they can wreak havoc. So this book will help those longing to grow in power evangelism develop in a way that is strengthening, encouraging and comforting.

However, this book is not only for those who want to grow in power evangelism. It is for anyone who wants to fully grasp the Gospel. I have come to believe that the majority of believers do not understand the Gospel, let alone know how to share it with others. This is why I will start off explaining what the Gospel is, before speaking of how to share it. I will show how God's love reaches out to us, and what that means for us.

When God's love and power begin to touch your heart, everything changes. Power evangelism is no longer a special activity; it becomes a way of life. So let's explore the power of His love.

CHAPTER 1

The Power of Love

> But while he was still a long way off, his father saw him and felt compassion, and ran and embraced him and kissed him.
> — LUKE 15:20

One day in Santarém, Brazil, pastor Abe Huber felt a familiar nudging. God had a task for him. He had to visit Gildo, a young man who sporadically came to his church. Come to think of it, he had not seen him in a while. Huber went to the man's house, knocked on the door, and Gildo's mother opened. Huber told her, "I'd like to speak to Gildo."

The mother disappeared to check with her son. When she came back, she did not have good news.

"Gildo does not want to see you."

Well, that was that, then. Huber was content; he could go home in the knowledge he had done his part. But just as he started to turn around, Gildo's mother added, "But I do want you to talk to him."

Huber followed the lady to Gildo's room and discovered why the man hadn't wanted to see him. Gildo had been too ashamed of his sins and addictions. Pastor Huber's response was simple: he gave him a fatherly embrace and told him, "God loves you so much! You are going to become a wonderful leader, a great man of God."

Gildo came back to church that Sunday and attended a new believers' Bible study. He even got baptized. But a month or so later he disappeared. Huber did not see him again for a long time. And when he finally reappeared in Huber's life, Gildo was walking down the street drunk.

Pastor Huber ran to him, hugged him and told him, "God loves you. He is going to use you mightily. You are going to become a very important leader."

Gildo was clearly moved to the core by the constant love and support that Pastor Huber continued to give him. He came to church that Sunday and this time, he kept coming. Pastor Gildo Vasconcelos is now one of the most important leaders of the PAZ movement[3] in Brazil. His life was transformed because Pastor Huber loved him with radical patience, tolerance and kindness. This is the kind of love that God loves us with (Rom. 2:4; Jonah 4:2).

In a parable rather like this story, Jesus likens the love of God to that of a father with two sons. The youngest abandons the father to live the high life. He spends his father's money until he finds himself not just feeding pigs, but also eating their food. At this low point, he decides to return to his father's house. He knows he no longer has rights there, so he plans to offer to work as a slave. But the welcome his father gives him shows outrageous love and forgiveness.

The story of the father's love is foundational for our faith and for the way we evangelize. Let's have a closer look at the text:

> But while he was still a long way off, his father *saw him* and felt *compassion*, and *ran* and *embraced* him and *kissed* him.
> – LUKE 15:20

There are five important lessons to be learned in how the father meets his son, and we will go through them one by one.[4]

His Father Sees Him

While the prodigal son is still a long way off, his father sees him. He is clearly on the lookout, eager for his son to return.

Like the father in the parable, God longs for us to come to Him. We were created because He wanted our friendship. In Genesis 1:26-27 we read a conversation that took place in the heavens. "Then God said, 'Let us make man in our image, after our likeness.' ... So God created man in his own image, in the image of God he created him; male and female he created them." We are made in the image of God, and our purpose is to interact with Him.

God not only longs for us, but He also sees us. He knows every single thing about us. He even knows how many hairs there are on our head (Luke 12:7)! God is love and He desires us with great passion and love.

One of the names God reveals himself by is "Jehovah El Roi", the God who sees me. Sarai's slave Hagar gets to know

Him by that name. When she flees Sarai's harsh treatment, an angel comes to her and tells her, "The LORD has listened to your affliction" (Gen. 16:11). The story then continues in verse 13, "She called the name of the LORD who spoke to her, 'You are a God of seeing,' for she said, 'Truly here I have seen him who looks after me.'" She knows: I am seen and I am looked after, because that is what God is like.

Even when we feel alone and think no one notices us, God sees us and He longs to be with us. Nothing can separate us from His love. And He sees for the people you meet in the street, too. He longs to be with them as well.

He Feels Compassion

When the prodigal is still a long way away, the father feels compassion. The word "compassion" literally means "to suffer with". God is not callous nor indifferent to injustice or suffering. In fact, at the heart of the Gospel is the story of His response to our suffering. Jesus Christ, God Himself, leaves heaven to become a man. He does so knowing that His destiny is to suffer and ultimately die a cruel death on the cross. Jesus does not have to go down this path, He does not deserve it. But He chooses to do it because He loves us. When He dies on that cross, He takes all the world's brokenness, sin and injustice upon Himself. It is the greatest act of self-sacrificial love and generosity in human history.

Jesus feels the pain of the people who have been robbed, tortured and abused in their minds and bodies. He became broken so that we could become whole (Isa. 53). He took upon himself our sins and brokenness. His words to us are:

> Come to me, all who labor and are heavy laden, and I will give you rest. Take my yoke upon you, and learn from me, for I am gentle and lowly in heart, and you will find rest for your souls. For my yoke is easy, and my burden is light.
> — MATTHEW 11:28-30

Jesus desires to take our burdens of hurt, pain and rejection. He desires to take away the pressure of having to perform and be "good." You will never have to wonder whether you are good enough when the Gospel of Jesus breaks into your heart. A life with God is a life of real rest and trust.

One day, while meditating on this scripture, I saw a picture of a woman with a backpack filled with hurt, pain and rejection. Clinging onto it, she said, "Nobody cares! Nobody loves me! I am nothing!"

While this woman clutched her backpack she jumped up and down, angry at God for not helping her. But then I saw Jesus standing before her saying, "Let Me take your backpack and give you a new one." The woman did not see Jesus (or want to see Him) and continued to rattle off her story of not being loved. The entire time Jesus stood there and said, "But I do love you and I want to take your burden. I want to give you My backpack, which is easy and light."

God cares. He is compassionate. Jesus' death and resurrection prove He loves us, not only with words, but with deeds. His died for the sins of all humanity past, present and future. Forgiveness is available for everyone. He does not want anyone to be lost. Yet, just like the woman with the backpack, God cannot force anyone to receive His love, peace and forgiveness.

Jesus, the Son of God, became human so that all of humanity could become sons and daughters of God. There is an exchange Jesus desires to make with us. If we give Him our lives, He wants to give us His. If we give Him our hurt, pain, sin and brokenness, He wants to give us healing, wholeness and a new identity and life.

He Runs to His Son

The father runs to his prodigal son. Likewise, our Father runs to us. His unfailing love and goodness *pursue* us all the days of our lives (Ps. 23:6, NLT). We love God "because he first loved us" (1 John 4:19). We are not an accident. We are desired and pursued.

There is a powerful parable of that pursuit in the Bible:

> The kingdom of heaven is like treasure hidden in a field, which a man found and covered up. Then in his joy he goes and sells all that he has and buys that field.
> — MATTHEW 13:44

Imagine what happened. A laborer is ploughing a field when he comes against something that seems like a large rock. As he digs deeper to remove the rock, he discovers a box full of ancient treasure.

He hides that box in the ground again and goes home to sell his car, stamp collection, iPhone, house ... everything! His family and neighbors worry about him and think he has gone crazy. He just replies, "Don't worry, I know what I'm doing."

The day finally comes where he has sold all of his belongings and can afford to buy the field where the treasure is hidden. When he finally gets to the field, he digs up the treasure and he is rich beyond his wildest dreams.

There are two legitimate ways to interpret this parable. One is that those who give up all their earthly belongings for the Kingdom of God will be highly rewarded. This is true (Matt. 6:33). Yet there is a second interpretation that also excites my heart. We are that hidden treasure. Jesus gave up all of the riches and comfort of heaven so that He could have us. We are God's treasure, the apple of his eye. We are what He most desires to have and when He has us, He is more than satisfied. This is why he is pursuing all of humanity"—so everyone can know Him.

He Embraces His Son

The father embraces the son. That is also what I do when I see my wife and children after a long time of being away: I take them in my arms. It is so wonderful to be touched, held and feel loved and wanted. Normally, my sons will ask me after that embrace, "So, what did you bring me?" Many parents work very hard to give their children material things and opportunities that they perhaps weren't able to have as a child. That is good, but it is so ironic that these things sometimes cost the children what they most desire: their parents' time and attention.

The father in Jesus' story gives his son great gifts: a new set of clothes, a ring, new shoes, an expensive feast to celebrate that he has returned. But what our heavenly Father longs to give most is Himself. He longs to embrace us and hold us close to His heart. Have you ever tried to hug someone who did not want to be hugged? It does not work very well. It's the same with us: to enjoy God's embrace, we must rest in it rather than wriggle away.

Our first dog that we had in Amsterdam was named Nena. Nena was my dog. She adored me and loved to lay on my lap while I rubbed her belly. There was nothing better in the world for Nena than being held and hugged by me. It was a very sad day for me when she passed away due to old age.

A year later, we got our next dog, Mia. She is a street dog rescued from Romania. When we first got her, Mia did not like to be hugged by me. She did not like me. She did love my children, however. She especially likes my oldest son. She was only interested in me when I had food. She simply didn't feel safe with me, most likely because of traumatic experiences she had with adult men. Slowly, my relationship with Mia is getting better. But being rejected by her has allowed me to experience something of what God feels when we reject Him. He desires to embrace us. At one time, Jesus expresses His longing like this: "How often would I have gathered your children together as a hen gathers her brood under her wings, and you were not willing!" (Matt. 23:37). We often just tell Him, "No, God, I am not interested in You or Your embrace."

He Kisses His Son

The father kisses his son. Likewise, God wants to kiss us. In the Song of Solomon 1:2, it says, "Let him kiss me with the kisses of his mouth!" Jewish rabbis interpret these kisses as a metaphor of the words that come from the mouth of God (Deut. 8:3). God wants to kiss you with His words. He wants you to know you are loved.

Giving people "kisses from God" is also a beautiful metaphor for sharing His words in power evangelism and prophetic ministry. I am continually amazed at how I see people react when God's love touches their hearts. I have seen people who consider themselves unbelievers on the streets of Amsterdam, Barcelona, Kiev, Budapest and elsewhere begin to tear up when we express God's love for them.

Being able to experience God's love for yourself is essential for that. One author wrote:

> You must try to pray so that, in your prayer, you open yourself in such a way that sometime—perhaps not today, but sometime—you are able to hear God say to you, "I love you!" These words, addressed to you by God, are the most important words you will ever hear because, before you hear

them, nothing is ever completely right with you, but after you hear them, something will be right in your life at a very deep level.[5]

Sharing the Father's love with people is what power evangelism is all about. Graham Cooke writes:

Ninety percent of prophecy is stating the obvious: God loves you, He cares for you, He wants the best for you, His kindness and faithfulness is with you. His love is eternal. He knows everything about your life. These are things every Christian knows and recites, but sometimes we get so locked into our circumstances that we lose sight of even those basic attributes of the character of God. We need to be reminded from time to time. We can read these same truths in Scripture, but sometimes we just need that "now" element of prophecy, allied to the Bible, to actually bring the word home to our circumstances in a dynamic way.[6]

The first time I consciously met a prophet, I was eleven years old. I remember him putting his hand on my shoulder and saying, "God loves you so much. You are really special to Him." For the next forty-eight hours I felt like I was in the hand of God. His presence was very tangible. This kiss of heaven was very real for me.

Granted, it is not necessary to feel God's presence and love all the time because we "walk by faith" and not by what we see or feel. (2 Cor. 5:7). Nevertheless, it is wonderful to experience God in our emotions, and we are called to love Him with all our hearts.

When God kisses us through His Word, everything changes. Our hearts, minds and bodies begin to experience what they have been made for. Love is the foundation upon which the Christian life is built. After all, when Jesus is asked what the most important of all commandments is, He says:

> You shall love the Lord your God with all your heart and with all your soul and with all your mind. This is the great and first commandment. And a second is like it: You shall love your neighbor as yourself. On these two commandments depend all the Law and the Prophets.
> — MATTHEW 22:37-40

This is often called the great commandment. There is another essential commandment in the Bible: the great commission. This is when Jesus says:

> Go therefore and make disciples of all nations, baptizing them in the name of the Father and of the Son and of the Holy Spirit, teaching them to observe all that I have commanded you. And behold, I am with you always, to the end of the age.
> — MATTHEW 28:19-20

Though the great commission is a Christian essential, we should never attempt to fulfill it if we are not first living out the great commandment. I've seen the damage that does. You may have seen similar examples. A young man would win over the hearts of women so they would sleep with him. If they had slept with him, he would cut off all connections with them. He was just using them for his ego and his satisfaction. Once he became a Christian, he became a small group Bible Study leader. Sounds great, right? But it soon became evident he felt the need to be in control all the time. He had to have the last say in everything that was said in the group. His behavior toward women had changed, but the root of his behavior had not changed yet. Pride and arrogance showed their face in another form: a religious one.

In the same way, people can do power evangelism, prophesy, heal the sick and cast out demons without being connected to Jesus (Matt. 7:20-23). People can have all the faith in the world and do great miracles, but if they do not do these things out of love then it is all worthless (1 Cor. 13:1-3).

Many times, people who have moved in a great "power" ministry also carried an "orphan" spirit. They don't experience God as a loving Father and so they quickly feel rejected or hurt. This can be very poisonous to the world and to the body of Christ. It is vital that those who want to move in God's power have their identity rooted and grounded in God's love. It is far more important than how many people they see accept Christ, how accurate they minister prophetically or how many people may get healed (Eph. 3:16-19). If your ministry is not rooted in God's love, it may well end up destroying other people and eventually yourself.

But if you are rooted in God's love, everything else will follow. So I want to finish this chapter by inviting you to read a letter I have written from God to you. Read this letter several times and meditate on it. What do you find difficult to receive? What feels true or untrue in your heart? Can you say, "God, I love You"? If you can, what does He say back?

My dear child,

You are of more value to Me than all the treasures of the entire earth (Matt. 13:44-45). I have paid the highest price for you (Col. 1:13-14). I chose you so that my Spirit can live inside of you. You are My temple and I live in you. I have chosen you as My home and I desire to live with you and in you (1 Cor. 6:19). Even though I am greater than all of the universe, I long to live inside of you.

You are my beloved child (1 John 3:1). I am very pleased with you and I love to sing over you as a father sings over his child (Zeph. 3:17). You are My passion, My inheritance, My treasure and in you I am well pleased.

You have captured My heart with one look of your eyes. Your love for Me is sweeter than wine (Song 4:9-10). I love you with an everlasting love. With My unfailing love I continue calling you to Myself (Jer. 31:3).

When you have been unfaithful to Me, I have continued to watch for you to come home (2 Tim. 2:13; Hos. 3:1-5). I desire to lead you with My bands of love (Hos. 11:3-4). I will take your yoke of weariness and pressure to perform from you and replace it with My yoke, which is easy and light (Matt. 11:28-30). I will lead you and give you true satisfaction and abundant life (John 10:10).

Even if everyone says that you must remain silent and quit talking to Me, I want you to speak to Me and ask Me for your heart's desire (Luke 18:41). I promise you that if you call to Me I will answer you, and will tell you great and hidden things that you have not known (Jer. 33:3). I have good plans for you, plans to give you a hope and a future. My plans for you are greater than you can think or imagine (Jer. 29:11; Eph. 3:20).

You are My masterpiece and we will do many things together (Eph. 2:10). Listen to and read My words. Let them sink into the depths of your heart so that My love can change your identity. I want to walk with you every day (Gen. 3:8). I know everything about you, even the number of hairs on your head. I know what you are going to say before you say it (Matt. 10:30; 6:8). Even so, I want you to talk to Me because I love to hear the sound of your heart.

I want to heal your heart and take away your sadness. I have begun a good work in you and I will complete it (Phil. 1:6). I come to you. I desire to be with you. You are My beloved. I see you. I feel your pain. I run to you, hug you and kiss you with My words. I will never leave you nor forsake you (Luke 15:20; Deut. 31:8).

I love you. I love you. I love you.

—***Your Daddy in Heaven***

POWER EVANGELISM — *JUST DO IT!*

QUESTIONS

1. Why do you think all power ministry must be based on love?

2. Have you ever seen someone share their faith well and effectively? Have you ever seen someone share their faith destructively? If so, what made the difference?

3. Three motivations to share your faith are 1) fear, 2) obligation or 3) love. Why is love more effective than the other two?

4. Can you say "I love you" to Father God? What does He say back to you? Is it easy for you to experience His love? Why or why not?

CHAPTER 2

The Gospel of Love

> See what kind of love the Father has given to us, that we should be called children of God; and so we are.
> — 1 JOHN 3:1

When Femke and I were just married, we were very happy, as just the two of us. And yet, there was something Femke yearned for. Something was missing. One Saturday morning after breakfast, Femke looked at me with a tear rolling down her cheek and told me, "Matthew, I want a baby." I thought this was a great idea. Having Judah, our firstborn, was a tremendous gift and addition to our family, as were his sister and brother, who came along a few years later. After nine years of marriage, however, I felt a yearning of my own; something I was missing. Having three children was great, but I looked at Femke and said, "Femke, I want another baby." That was when God sent us our youngest boy, Benjamin.

I love all of my children equally, yet there was something special about my relationship with Benjamin. Femke began working as a pre-school teacher, and I got to spend one or two whole days a week with my Benjamin. We went to the zoo in Amsterdam. We went to special playgrounds. We went on long bike rides. Having those "papa" days with Benjamin created a deep bond with him. For many years, the first person Benjamin would come to was his papa, not his mama. Whenever I left on long trips, he would ball his eyes out because he missed his papa.

In many ways, the relationship I enjoy with Benjamin, and my other children, is like the relationship we can have with God.

Paul describes it in this way:

> For all who are led by the Spirit of God are sons of God. For you did not receive the spirit of slavery to fall back into fear, but you have received the Spirit of adoption as sons, by whom we cry, "Abba! Father!" The Spirit himself bears witness with our spirit that we are children of God ...
> — ROMANS 8:14-16

The Spirit of God inside of us cries out to Father God saying, "*Abba!*" (see Rom. 8:15). This Aramaic word is an intimate and very personal word that can be translated as *papa* or *daddy*. My children call me papa or daddy, and share their joys, sorrows and worries with me. We enjoy spending time together. The good news of the Bible is that we can know God in a similar, intimate way. Every voice of fear and worry in our mind and hearts can be replaced with God's voice. He will tell us, "You are my dearly beloved child. I am pleased with you. You are My child and I am your Papa!"

Knowing God as our *Abba* transforms our thinking. God replaces our harmful, insecure, broken thought patterns with His deep security and love. This sets us free. One lady we know can testify to this. We had helped her get out of prostitution. Once, she spent some time in her country of origin. Feeling bored and depressed, she began contemplating returning to a life of partying and drunkenness. She thought, "Pastor Mateo is not here and I can do whatever I want. It does not matter."

That night, she had a dream where she was racing a jeep into a valley, toward a cliff. She slammed on the brakes and then started climbing out of the valley. She said, "I am not going back to my old life! I am not going down this way anymore!"

In her dream, she heard God using my voice to say to her, "You are my dearly beloved daughter. I am so happy with you."

When she woke up, she decided she would never return to her old life. As she reflected upon her past, she realized her motivation for working in prostitution so many years was to earn her mother's love. If she could buy her mother a car and a house, her mother would love her and approve of her. But she did not need her mother's approval anymore, she now had God's.

To her amazement, on that same trip, her mother told her how much she loved her and how proud she was of her. She realized she did not need money, parties, or alcohol to be happy. She now had God's love, and that was enough. The change in her life has been awesome to watch.

Religion or Relationship?

Though God invites us to a Father-and-child relationship, we often feel we have to earn his love. This is what this book calls "religion": following a set of laws to obey in order to be acceptable to God. It is righteousness based on rules. When Jesus walked on earth, He often fought with religion. He rebuked the Pharisees, the religious elite, but spoke kindly to the rulebreakers. He said, "Those who are well have no need of a physician, but those who are sick. Go and learn what this means: 'I desire mercy, and not sacrifice.' For I came not to call the righteous, but sinners" (Matt. 9:12-13). What Jesus preached was not a rulebook, but a relationship.

After a church service, a woman came up to me and said, "I have been a Christian all my life but now I am doubting everything. All I have believed has been based on obligation and fear." My answer was, "That is wonderful news!" To grow, we need to unlearn incorrect things so that we can learn correct things. That's a painful but healthy process. A faith based on obligation and fear is not healthy. It is religion, not relationship. It is legalism, not the Gospel. The voice speaking through it is the accuser's, not God's. When this woman gets to know God as a caring Father who loves her unconditionally, it will set her free.

Religion pressurizes people to work hard so they can earn God's love and favor. Pray more! Study the Bible more! Go to church more! Fast more! Do more! There is no end to the list. There is nothing wrong with praying long or reading the Bible a lot, but the motivation to do so is wrong. No matter how hard you try, religion keeps telling you you're not doing enough, you are not enough. Religion says, "I messed up. God is angry at me." Relationship says, "I messed up. I want to run to Papa God."

One day, I discovered one of my children was struggling with religious thinking. This child was having a very difficult time. Some heart-to-heart exchange was needed. This child began crying and told me, "Papa, I am a horrible person because I am a sinner and have done really bad things."

I quieted my child and said, "Why don't you silence yourself and talk to Papa God and ask Him what He thinks of you?"

My child was quiet for a moment, and then said, "I hear two voices that tell me something totally different."

I said, "Well, what do you hear?"

"The first voice says I am His beloved child and that He loves me very much."

I said, "Yes, that is the true voice of Papa God. What does the other voice say?"

"The other voice says I am a sinner and that I am no good." Tears started flowing upon hearing this voice of condemnation, judgment and unfair criticism.

My child was hearing the voice of religion, not the message of Jesus Christ. Unfortunately, many believers (and non-believers) believe this voice represents the Gospel. That is why many people do not want to have anything to do with the Church, the Gospel and evangelism.

Evangelizing based on religion isn't sharing the Gospel of Jesus, but giving bad news. The message preached may be inspired by fear, accusation and ultimately by Satan himself. After all, he is the one who accuses and condemns us (Rev. 12:9-11; Zech. 3:1).

As a teenager, my youth group and I went to a Marilyn Manson[7] concert venue to pray and share Jesus with concertgoers. There, we were confronted with two other groups of Christians who were sharing their faith in opposite ways.

The first group had a large bullhorn and a banner with a picture of hell on it. They blared at everyone going into the concert that they were destined to go to that place. The second group of Christians had a very different strategy. They were dressed in black and looked like any other concertgoer. They engaged people in conversation and I saw how they actually got to share about Jesus and pray with different concertgoers. These groups' methods and results were extremely different.

In the meantime, no one was willing to talk to our youth group, because we were dressed in normal clothes and the concertgoers thought we belonged to that first group of Christians with their bullhorn and banner.

The climax of the evening was when a woman from the group with the "hell" banner confronted this other Christian woman: she was going to hell because she was wearing a black T-shirt. I did some profound soul-searching about evangelism after this. How in the world could sharing the Gospel result in relegating someone to hell because of the color of their shirt? If it is the most wonderful, amazing, life-changing and exhilarating news in the world, why were Christians acting in this way? And why did so many attempts to share the Gospel not connect with people's hearts and minds?

This is what I have come to believe: evangelism is so much more than just winning an argument and praying a prayer. It is being connected to God and helping others connect to His reality. When they do, lives are changed and people flourish because they find what they have always longed for. The Gospel is so much more than simply knowing four points and praying a prayer. It is knowing God Himself. It is having a two-way relationship with Him that radically changes every part of our being. The Gospel is dynamic: it never stops changing our hearts and affects every area of our lives.

Just to be clear: I am by no means superior to those who are under the influence of religion. All our hearts go in that direction, including mine. Following the voice of legalistic religion with its clear rulebook is easier than developing an intimate relationship with God. Our hearts search for a way to earn His favor by simply doing the right things without having to be dependent on Him. But God has something much more beautiful for us.

Truth and Grace

In Exodus 19, God describes the kind of intimate relationship He wants to have with His people. He says:

> You yourselves have seen what I did to the Egyptians, and how I bore you on eagles' wings and brought you to myself. Now therefore, if you will indeed obey my voice and keep my covenant, you shall be my treasured possession among all peoples, for all the earth is mine; and you shall be to me a kingdom of priests and a holy nation.
> – EXODUS 19:4-6

God wants a close relationship with the Israelites. They should know that they are treasured and holy. They should be priests: knowing God, bringing earth to heaven and heaven to earth. However, this is not the kind of relationship Israel chooses to have with God. They actually end up telling Moses, "You speak to us, and we will listen; but do not let God speak to us, lest we die" (Ex. 20:19). Time and time again, God's people ignore Him and live their own self-centered and self-righteous lives based on their own performance and so-called goodness. This breaks His heart.

But God says:

> Behold, the days are coming, declares the LORD, when I will make a new covenant with the house of Israel and the house of Judah ...
> – JEREMIAH 31:31

He promises He will put His "law within them, and ... write it on their hearts" (Jer. 31:33a). He says:

> I will be their God, and they shall be my people. And no longer shall each one teach his neighbor and each his brother, saying, 'Know the LORD,' for they shall all know me, from the least of them to the greatest, declares the LORD. For I will forgive their iniquity, and I will remember their sin no more.
> — JEREMIAH 31:33-34

This new covenant, this new way of relating to us, is through Jesus Christ. The apostle John describes it in this way: "For from his fullness we have all received, grace upon grace. For the law was given through Moses; grace and truth came through Jesus Christ" (John 1:16-17). Truth and grace are at the heart of the Gospel.

Truth without grace causes me to do good things such as study the Bible, pray, go to church, evangelize so that God can be happy with me. The Gospel leads to me do those same good things because God is happy with me and I am so happy with Him. Truth without grace leads me to be a slave to insecurity and fear. I never know if I have done enough. The Gospel allows me to live in freedom because I live with my Papa God. Truth without grace leads me to live for God and the Gospel to live with God. Truth without grace leads me to pray to get things from God and the Gospel leads me to pray simply because I get to be with my Papa God. The one causes me to be a human doing, the other allows me to live as human being.

Truth without grace is all about believing and doing the right things in order to be good. It imposes rules upon us to change us from the outside in. The resulting fear, guilt and a sense of obligation can change our behavior, but they cannot change our hearts and make us like Jesus Christ. This is why concepts such as radical love, mercy, forgiveness and grace are so intrinsic to the Gospel message. The Gospel changes us from the inside out.

Graceful Living

What does it look like if your evangelism models grace? Some stories from our church community may shed some light on that. One of our visitors comes from a transgender background. The only experience she had of attending church was when she walked in and immediately the pastor began preaching against homosexuality and condemning homosexuals. Everyone in the church knew that he was talking about her. All of her life, she had had suicidal thoughts. Then she was diagnosed with cancer and was certain that she was going to die. During her last trip to her country or origin, she actually said goodbye to everyone, sure her life was almost over. But she began coming to our church and has been getting to know Jesus. She is now free of cancer and the desire to die has been replaced with a great desire to live. Her time of praise and worship is very special to her and we have watched how Jesus is changing her life. She has a peace she never experienced before, and she continually brings new people to our church.

The subject of gender and homosexuality is a charged, polarized and political one. Often, when those who are transgender come to our church they ask me if they have to cut off their hair and have their breasts removed in order to be welcome. I reply that everyone is welcome as they are in our church. God does love us as we are; yet His love does not leave us as we are. It changes us from the inside out.

The worst thing I can do is to place conditions on people coming to church and hearing the Gospel. It is as we hear the Gospel and it touches our hearts that our lives are changed. People may change temporarily if I tell them they have to, but real transformation takes place when God, through his love, truth and grace changes them from the inside out. If people cannot come to our churches to hear the Gospel, then where can they go?

Too often we focus on people's outward appearance or lifestyle instead of focusing on their hearts – as God does. We do not see them as precious sons and daughters, dearly loved by God. Subjects such as gender and sexuality are important, but they can become distractions from sharing and knowing the Gospel. Get to know Jesus' love and power first and then speak to Him about secondary subjects such as sexuality.

One friend of mine had a homosexual lifestyle for many years and when he became a Christian was concerned that people would try to take him through "conversion therapy" to undo his homosexual feelings. This never happened. Instead, as he got to know Christ more and more, he began surrendering every area of his life to Jesus Christ, including his sexuality. To his surprise, he fell in love with a woman and at the time of writing is considering marriage. This is not something people demanded he do before he could become a Christian. Instead, as he drew closer to God, his desires began changing.

This is a highly sensitive, complicated and emotionally charged subject that I cannot fully address nor understand completely. But I know we should not discriminate when sharing God's love and power with people. Jesus died for all of us and everyone deserves to be loved as God loves us. We should treat people with respect, no matter what faith, culture or background they come from.

Every week when we visit those working in the Red-Light District, my message for them is not one of condemnation – I am not telling them they are living in sin. Condemnation destroys, but the conviction of the Holy Spirit gives life. I declare their true identity and the destiny that God has for them. I share the Gospel with truth and grace, as Jesus did (John 1:17).

Most weeks, I listen to people working in prostitution telling me how terrible it is and how difficult it is to leave it; they desire to get out, but they just don't know how. Then it is our job to help them develop a plan to make a career switch. Change works best when it is driven by their own desire and not because we try to impose it upon them. In that case, change is rarely permanent.

Of course, there are times to speak about sin and brokenness. But it is important that our preaching is more Christ-centered than sin-centered. Because it is Christ's love that transforms lives.

The Bride Who Cost Eight Cows

Let me illustrate this with a story I read about a tribe in the South Pacific Islands where dowries were payed for brides.[8] If you wanted to marry a very beautiful woman, you would pay a five-cow dowry. If she was pretty, but not excessively so, four cows. If she was just plain and ugly, three cows would do.

Two men heard that the wealthiest businessman on the island had given an eight-cow dowry for the ugliest woman in the area. Their curiosity concerning this transaction led them to decide to visit this businessman to see if this was really true. They paddled their boats to the man's residence and knocked on his door. The man let them come in and seated them in his living room. Then he started calling his wife: "My dear, lovely wife, will you please bring some cookies and teas to our guests?" She responded by coming to the living room.

As the door opened, one man ribbed his friend and whispered, "Ugliest woman? Eight cows!"

To their amazement, in walked the most beautiful woman they had ever seen. The woman everyone had labeled as unattractive and of little value was transformed when her husband told her and showed her she was beautiful and precious. Her life was changed from the inside out.

The story of the eight cows has important lessons for us. We were not purchased by eight, nine or ten cows. We were bought with Jesus' life. Jesus sacrificed His life for us, even though we were his enemies, so that we could become His beloved (Rom. 5:8-10). When we experience God's love and grace, we are transformed from the inside out. The Gospel changes everything.

It is God's kindness, tolerance and patience that leads us to repentance (Rom. 2:4, NLT). It is God's grace that "[trains] us to renounce ungodliness and worldly passions, and to live self-controlled, upright and godly lives in this present age" (Titus 2:12).

The Gospel saves lives but religion destroys it. What is motivating you in your relationship with God and with others? What is your motivation to share the Gospel?

POWER EVANGELISM—*JUST DO IT!*

QUESTIONS

1. How can you avoid treating people as "evangelism projects" and coming across as a used car salesman?

2. How does the Gospel change us from the inside out instead of from the outside in?

3. How important is it that we share the gospel using truth and grace?

4. What does God really think about "sinners?" What does He really think about you? Why are your answers important for the way you share the Gospel?

5. How is sharing the Gospel different than just bothering people? How does the Gospel change and improve people's lives?

CHAPTER 3

How People Come to Christ

> To change governing ideas, whether for individuals or for a group, is one of the most difficult and painful things in human life. Genuine conversion is a wrenching experience. It rarely happens ... except in the form of divine intervention, revolution or something very likely to a mental breakdown.[9]
> – DALLAS WILLARD

In many places, evangelism has a bad reputation. It is associated with being a rude, arrogant know-it-all. People confuse evangelism with selling legalistic religion. Nothing could be further from the truth. Let me illustrate it this way. In Amsterdam, there is a severe shortage of housing. Small rooms or apartments might cost astronomic sums of money. We are constantly asked by people whether we can help them find a home. To be honest, this task seems nearly impossible. But what if we had a way to find a home for everyone who needed one? To them, that would be good news (Gospel). If we could help everyone find an affordable house, we would be well-known, loved and searched after by everyone. That's basically what evangelism is all about: helping people find their heart's true home in Christ.

Jesus offers true fulfillment, satisfaction and life that the world cannot offer. When we share the Gospel, we are not disrespecting or diminishing people, we are aiming at giving them something immensely valuable and adding value to their lives. We are helping them find their hearts' desires in Christ.

However, it often takes time for people to discover their heart's home in Christ. It is a process of overcoming the things hindering them: their prejudices, cynicism and fear. Let's examine Maria's[10] story as an example.

> Almost a year ago, I started the Alpha course at the Hellands' home. I didn't know what to think of it. Here's the picture: A twenty-six-year-old girl, insecure about social engagement, walks into a house full of strangers. That is sure to shut down the heart. But there I met a woman oozing niceness. Also, a man who looks too young to have the three kids who curiously jump around the house and hug the people in it. The Helland family has opened their house to welcome me.
>
> It's the perfect stereotype of Christianity. It's a play, well-performed. It's pretty on the outside, but can't be real on the inside. And yet, it is worth a shot. I want to know what they are going to tell me, right? So I do what I always do when I don't know what to think or feel: I tell myself to sit it out and then say my polite thanks.
>
> But something happens during that night. There is this one moment where my whole body is filled with an energy I can only call love. And I am thinking and wondering: how can this be? Here, I hear things I've known to be true all my life. Here is the story of love, peace and healing;

> the story of rebuilding yourself; the story of unconditional love and care for people; here is the story of my heart! Only they talk about Jesus and claim He is the truth, the way and the life. I have never found an answer for my beliefs, but claiming it lies in Jesus? No. That simply cannot be. It just can't. That is something for Christians, not for me.
>
> Today, the day I am writing this, is the last day of my second round of Alpha: almost a year after that first evening where the play was performed and the pretty picture on the outside turned out to be real. I have lost my flat, one-dimensional perspective of the Helland family and Christianity. In its place I have gained a vibrant, three-dimensional perspective of God. And the Helland family? They've shown the stereotype of Christianity being fake and superficial as untrue. It couldn't be more real.
>
> There is so much more to say, but through the Helland family, and of course through the Uncreated, I feel like I have been welcomed back home.

Maria's journey to Christ was in progress. Her faith was growing. However, getting to the point of being baptized and publicly confessing Him as her Lord and Savior would take more time. We will read more about how that developed later.

Conversion is rarely a one-off response to a one-time event. As Timothy Keller has explained: "Research shows that the more varied ways a person hears the Gospel, and the more often a person hears the Gospel before making a commitment, the better the comprehension, the less likely 'reversion' to the world is."[11] In other words, the more often people hear and understand the Gospel, the more chances it will have of sticking and influencing every area of their lives.

One Iranian woman I know met a Christian in downtown Amsterdam when she first came to the Netherlands. She allowed this Christian to pray with her. She had no idea what she did, but that memory stuck with her. A few years later, an Iranian evangelist shared the Gospel with her. However, she decided she would never become a Christian. Then someone told her about a man who would be preaching at a local church with a gift of prophecy and healing—me. She went, and at that service, I prophesied over her. Her back was healed after I prayed for it. She began coming to our church, but told me that she did not want to be baptized. A few weeks later, though, she started having dreams where I was baptizing her and she was following Christ. Two months later, I baptized her and now she often makes up part of my prophetic ministry team when I travel.

The prayer this woman prayed in downtown Amsterdam was very important, but not the conclusion of her journey toward knowing Christ. It was the beginning of a journey that will continue for the rest of her life.

Starting Points

Where people are in the process of conversion can be illustrated by means of The Gray Matrix (Extended).[12]

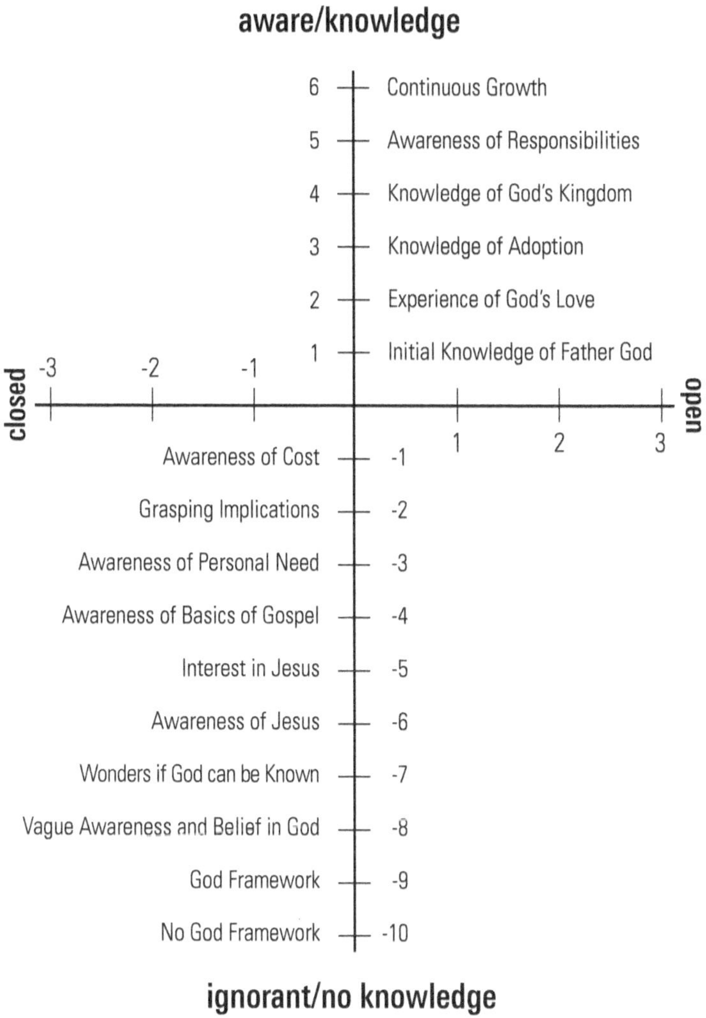

HOW PEOPLE COME TO CHRIST

aware/knowledge

6	Continuous Growth
5	Awareness of Responsibilities
4	Knowledge of God's Kingdom
3	Knowledge of Adoption
2	Experience of God's Love
1	Initial Knowledge of Father God

closed -3 -2 -1 | 1 2 3 **open**

Awareness of Cost	-1
Grasping Implications	-2
Awareness of Personal Need	-3
Awareness of Basics of Gospel	-4
Interest in Jesus	-5
Awareness of Jesus	-6
Wonders if God can be Known	-7
Vague Awareness and Belief in God	-8
God Framework	-9
No God Framework	-10

ignorant/no knowledge

The further below zero a person is regarding their knowledge of God, the less they know or think about God. A minus ten on the chart means that they have absolutely no idea that God exists. A minus seven means that they believe God exists, but are unsure whether they could really know Him. A zero on the chart means that they have made a decision to live with Christ. A positive five speaks about taking responsibility as a believer—it is going toward mature faith.

This chart's horizontal line also has a positive and a negative side. People on the negative end of this line may know a lot or very little about the Gospel, but they are not open to hearing more about Him. People on the positive end may know a lot or very little, and they are open to finding out more. This chart helps you to figure out where people you are talking to are, regarding knowing more about Christ.

When I am in places such as Mexico, Chile, Brazil or Ukraine, I find that people are very open to talking about God. In a Western European context, people are generally a lot more closed or even hostile when someone tries to talk to them about God. However, in the past decade, I have noticed a change. When I first arrived in Holland in 2005, people weren't very open to hearing about God. Now, especially the young are open. They may see themselves as "spiritual" and may believe in "something" but often know very little or nothing about the Bible and the Gospel. It is so much fun to tell a Bible story and notice people are curious to find out what happens in the end.

In some parts of the world, like the south of the USA, there are church buildings of all shapes and sizes on nearly every corner. In my parents' home town of Tulsa, Oklahoma, for example, there are many churches with anywhere between ten and twenty-five thousand members. Some are even bigger. Every time I visit the place now, I experience culture shock, because there are churches and Christians everywhere I go.

I remember going to get my driver's license renewed and everyone in the waiting room was a Christian. Some people were even studying their Bibles while waiting. I got into my car and heard all of the different Christian radio stations. It is just a completely different spiritual reality from in my neighbourhood in Amsterdam, where the most common religion is Islam. In the whole of the Netherlands, things are very different. In 1897, 97 percent of the population were members of a church. Now, in my city, only 3 percent of people consider themselves to be Christians. And compared to many other parts of Europe, this is actually a high percentage. So in large swathes of Europe, people don't not know a lot about God, the Bible and the meaning of the Gospel. In addition, they may not even be willing to talk about it.

Kickstarting the Process

When people aren't naturally open to hearing the Gospel, power evangelism can break down their barriers. If I am able to give a word of knowledge or show how God still heals, these same people often very become more open and interested in hearing what I have to say about the Gospel. This can kickstart the process of conversion.

In the Netherlands, the Church is the most distrusted of all institutions.[13] Many people associate the word "Church" with sexual abuse, manipulation, corruption, persecution and discrimination. In this context, rather than starting a conversation about Christianity and the Church, wouldn't it be better to begin a conversation with a demonstration of God's power if you want to share the Gospel? Jesus and His disciples used healing, words of knowledge, deliverance and prophecy to preach the Gospel; so these tools are still available today for us to share the Gospel.

A good friend of mine, Juriaan Beek, once walked up to two people and asked them if he could give them a demonstration of God's love and power. They responded by mocking him. Beek then simply asked one of them whether he was suffering from pain in his right ankle. The man was, and after Beek prayed for him, all the pain disappeared. This gave Beek a credibility and authority he did not have before using the word of knowledge and the healing. He was able to get their attention and share the Gospel.

Another friend of mine has just had a similar experience. A man came to sell her a lottery ticket. She told him she had found her fortune already by getting to know Jesus, but he just responded he did not believe in God. She gave him a word of knowledge describing a situation going on in his life and how he was feeling. He started crying, and she was able to share more about knowing Jesus. She even got to pray with him.

When evangelizing, I often find that the moment I begin using words of knowledge and simply speaking out God's love over people, they begin to cry. Using the gifts of the Spirit this way often enables us to bypass the intellectual barriers people have and speak directly to their hearts.

One Saturday, I went to the local shopping centre to talk to people about the Gospel. On the way there, I asked God for a name of a person I was going to meet. A name came to mind, but I was not convinced, and said, "God, You have told me that name before. It has to be me making this up." An hour later, I met a woman with that same name. When I started telling her that God was speaking to me about her earlier that day, the tears started flowing. God gave me words of life to speak over her and she gladly prayed and talked to Jesus. We did not simply have a rational conversation about Jesus, she spoke to Jesus and He touched her with this love and His word.

All-Round Evangelism

Effective evangelism takes an all-round approach, keeping in mind the intellectual, personal, social, spiritual and cultural dimension of sharing the Gospel. Let's go through these one by one.

Firstly, the *intellectual* dimension. It is important that people can understand the Gospel. I would be seen as crazy if I told people three hundred years ago green aliens came to the earth and if we believed in them our lives would be transformed. But this story may be exactly how some people hear us when we talk about our faith in Jesus Christ. That is why people need to hear the Gospel repeatedly in different ways before they can make an intellectual and rational decision.

Though the Gospel is not complicated, it has many layers and dimensions. The Bible is full of stories and principles giving us more insight into the Gospel. Never stop learning how you can share the Gospel with people so they can understand it. Never stop experimenting and trying out different ways to share the Gospel.

Understanding the Gospel also requires getting rid of stereotypes. When people hear the word "God" they may have a whole range of different associations. Some imagine a Gandalf-like character with a long white beard and a big staff, who is ready to hit us with it if we misbehave. Others envisage a Santa Clause figure who knows when we are sleeping or awake and whether we have been good enough to deserve presents. They think the goal of all religions is simply to "be good" and "be happy." But the Gospel of Jesus Christ is so much more than simply being "good."

Timothy Keller uses the term "defeater beliefs" for these types of stereotypes and misunderstandings about Christianity. Defeater beliefs impede people from giving the Gospel a fair hearing. He defines these defeater beliefs as "a set of beliefs a culture believes to be 'common sense' which make Christianity implausible. Every culture has different ones, but when there are many, it will be difficult for the Gospel to get a hearing in that culture."[14]

It is human to merely repeat what we have heard other people say, without much deep thought. That is why it is good to think things through and have an answer ready when people ask hard questions. But also recognize that your ability to share the Gospel does not hinge on being able to have all the answers to the world's most difficult question. Evangelism is not only an exercise in rational logic and philosophy, it is also an exercise in communicating the heart and thoughts of God. It is an exercise in love and learning to simply share Christ in you (Col. 1:27).

Secondly, the *personal* dimension. People don't hear the Gospel in a vacuum; their life experiences influence how they interpret its message. Those who have suffered because of the hypocrisy or dishonesty of Christians will see things from that perspective. They won't be very open to learning more about Christ. My grandfather, for example, never wanted to go to church because there were so many Christians who owed him money.

It is essential to listen to people's stories and not assume to know where they stand. Evangelism is never simply a formula —having the right answers for everybody's questions. Listen to God and listen to people as they speak to you.

There are two extremes to avoid when sharing the Gospel. One is being afraid to say or do anything because you fear giving offence. The other is just going through the "evangelistic program" without sensitivity to the other's personal situation. You are an ambassador for Christ, so talk to people while listening to God and to them. Courageously share the Gospel, and do so in a fashion that honours God and the people you are talking to. Your goal, after all, is to get them closer to making an informed decision for Christ. I have led people in a prayer to accept Christ, but then realized they have no clue what they just did. This is not ideal.

Thirdly, the *social* dimension. People tend to socialize with people who look and think like they do. When our church in Amsterdam had few teenagers, my children liked going to another church's youth group to be with people of their own age. The social dimension can pose challenges – for people from certain religious backgrounds it can be very difficult to become a Christian because of pressure from their families and communities. It can also be a force for good, when new churches are planted in specific communities or people groups. In a church community, people see how to apply the Gospel to their daily lives among people whose challenges are just like theirs.

Fourthly, the *spiritual* dimension. Let me start with an example. One day, I was sitting on a bench in downtown Amsterdam praying over one of my friends when suddenly I felt a half-liter of Pepsi soak my jeans. I looked up and there was a young man who spat at me and flipped me off. What was so odd about that encounter was that I was not speaking to him at all. I suspect that there was something spiritual in his hatred toward what I was saying and doing.

We would be naïve to not recognize that there is a spiritual battle going on when we talk to people about Christ. Paul wrote:

> In their case the god of this world has blinded the minds of the unbelievers, to keep them from seeing the light of the gospel of the glory of Christ, who is the image of God.
> – 2 CORINTHIANS 4:4

In traveling around different parts of the world, I am astounded by different cultures' receptivity to and acceptance of the Gospel. Some cultures are more open to giving the Gospel a fair hearing than others. In places like South Korea, Ukraine and Brazil, the Church has grown considerably in the past one hundred and twenty years, while in Western Europe, the decline of Christianity has been staggering. Though the reasons for this are many, spiritual forces are at the heart of it. Western European culture has adopted a set of beliefs making Christianity's claims seem irrelevant or dangerous to the world's freedom and happiness. It requires patience, prayer and creativity to communicate the Gospel to such a culture that doesn't think it needs to hear it.

All cultures have their own characteristics. The French are good cooks, the Germans build great cars, and Dutch are fantastic entrepreneurs. God has placed these redemptive traits in their cultures' DNA. Yet at the same time, dark spiritual forces can lead entire cultures astray, blinding them to evil. Different cultures have opened doors to different spiritual forces by worshiping "false gods." This can be seen clearly in places such as Syria, where in the name of radical Islam people were tortured, murdered and raped. It is evident in Japan, where suicide is a normal occurrence and in Mexico, where "death" is literally worshiped and murder is far too common.

Spiritual forces are fighting to keep people from hearing and understanding the Gospel. Evangelism has great consequences in the spiritual world. We will see people's bodies healed through prayer. And more than that: their spiritual eyes will be opened so they can understand and make a decision to follow Jesus (2 Cor. 4:4). This is why prayer is such an integral part of sharing the Gospel with people.

Many methods of evangelism focus on giving a rational presentation of the Gospel, but prayer is the hammer breaking down spiritual strongholds. Before, during and after we share the Gospel with people, we should pray. The old axiom says, "Do not talk to people about God until you have talked to God about those people." By the way, you can talk to God about people even while you are talking to those people.

Fifthly, the *cultural* dimension. When working with people from a variety of backgrounds, recognize that different cultures have their own questions and concerns that are answered by the Gospel. For example, many Asian cultures see the world in terms of shame and honor. Can you present the Gospel in a way that shows that Jesus frees us from all shame and fills us with honor?

In contemporary African cultures, a major question is how to be freed from evil forces. People in many parts of Africa are acutely aware of witchcraft and demons. Can you share and validate the Gospel by demonstrating that Jesus is more powerful than any demon? Can you help free people of demonic oppression? Can you heal the sick? Many ministers from a Western background with no training in deliverance or healing are ill-equipped to answer such questions. But these are important subjects when presenting the Gospel effectively in an African context.

The primary question most evangelistic methods answer is: "How can I be forgiven of my sins?" This is an excellent question in Western moral-based individualistic cultures. Especially in pockets of the world that still see themselves as "Christian" and have respect and some knowledge of the Bible.

However, in a postmodern expressive, individualistic culture, like the one prevalent in Western Europe, few people worry about how they can be forgiven of their sins. They do not necessary believe in God, heaven or sin. Instead, people's highest value is freedom. The question that the Gospel best answers in this context is: "How can I find true freedom?"

In Dutch, a common saying is *"vrijheid blijheid"* (freedom is happiness), and yet many people suffer from depression, burnout and even thoughts of suicide. Many young Dutch people have turned to yoga, mindfulness and other "spiritual" practices to fill their inner need for peace. As Christians, we know a peace that "surpasses all understanding" (Phil. 4:7). We know the source of true joy and freedom. Our task is to live that out and share it.

No matter what context you are in, it is important to be like Paul, who became all things to all people. To the Jew he was a Jew and to those who were not Jews, he became like them (1 Cor. 9:20-21). So we need to learn how people think and act when sharing the Gospel. Our goal in evangelizing is never just transferring information, but sharing truth and grace that will lead to transformation.

How to Evangelize

There is no one way to share the Gospel. Even in the Bible, we read of many ways. Peter and Paul are fantastic at direct preaching and reasoning (Acts 2:14-42; 17:2). A blind man knows very little about Christ, but he shares his personal testimony of how he was blind and now he can see (John 9:25). Matthew invites all of his friends to eat at meal at his house (Matt. 9:10-17). Dorcas is known for taking care of the poor and serving others (Acts 9:36). The Samaritan woman at the well shares what Jesus has said to her with the people of her village (John 4:39-42). All of the apostles use the power of God when they share the Gospel (Acts 2:43). No matter how God may use you to share the Gospel, here are three tips.

1. Just be you – Be normal, honest and genuine. Don't feel pressure to perform or be something you are not. God's power works best when we are at peace, so relax and listen to God and to people. When you find or can create an opening to share your testimony, pray or explain the Gospel, just do it.

A Dutch couple discovered the power of just being themselves after they came to a living faith in Jesus Christ while living in Canada. They immediately booked a flight back to their home country to witness to all their family members. They spent ten days there, staying up late every night trying to convince them to believe in Christ. No one accepted Christ. Six months later, however, the husband's youngest brother told them he chosen to give his life to Christ. Excited, the man asked his brother what argument had convinced him to follow Christ. His brother answered he did not remember anything he was told, he simply recalled the peace and joy he saw in his sister-in-law's face. One night he prayed to God and asked Him if he could have what she had. His life was totally transformed.

Evangelism is not just sharing the Gospel with words, it is who you are. If the Gospel is at the core of your identity, evangelism ceases to be something you only do and becomes something you naturally are.

2. Don't talk too long – Learn to be concise and don't feel like you have to preach Genesis to Revelation. When I was a teenager, I drove young people to a church event in the church van. I had a captive audience and I told them all I had to say. I succeeded in preaching, but I did not really connect with them at all. Do share what you have to say, but do it in a fashion that you are connecting with your hearers.

3. *Don't give up!* – When we started sharing the Gospel in Amsterdam's Red-Light District, Femke and I encountered people who did not want to talk to us. Those same people are now followers of Christ. It is challenging, but highly rewarding when we are able to develop a friendship with someone who previously did not even want to talk to us. One woman told me, "Pastor Mateo, when you first started, nobody wanted to talk to you. Now, every Tuesday there are women waiting for you to come pray for them." Don't give up on people. After all, God never gives up on us!

Maria's Decision

Earlier, we read Maria's testimony after a year of coming to our home and taking part in two Alpha courses. She was close to becoming a Christian, but still did not feel ready to be baptized. That moment came one evening at a youth meeting in a very special way.

Maria accompanied me and some others to a youth group where I was going to teach on prophecy. When I arrived, the faith in the atmosphere was noticeably low. I remember how Maria stood there, her arms crossed, and said, "You know, I really need to know if God exists."

Several of the young men present were Muslims and one asked me why I had such a strange accent when speaking Dutch. I tried to teach on prophecy, but there was no interest at all.

I then began to prophesy over everyone present and the faith levels shot up. People's eyes got very big as I began describing their lives and things of their past, present and possible future. The presence of God became very tangible in the room.

Toward the end of the meeting, I challenged everyone to ask God to speak to them personally. Everyone present, including Maria and the Muslim men, experienced God speaking to them directly and through others in the room. (This is actually similar to a situation Paul describes in 1 Corinthians 14:24-25).

Maria ended the evening with tears coming down her face as she heard the living God speaking to her. A week or two later, I baptized her.

Evangelism is a process that takes time, prayer, love, faith and commitment. We must have courage and sensitivity to connect God's story with people's story. It can feel terrifying and difficult, yet it is thrilling to see people's hearts and lives changed by the Gospel.

Evangelism is not a about a method or religion, but about getting to know a living, powerful and loving God. We don't have to do so out of our own strength; God gives us authority and power. More on that in the next chapter!

POWER EVANGELISM—*JUST DO IT!*

EXERCISE
Intercession

Make a list of five people who don't know Christ yet. Place that list where you will see it every day, and pray for them often. I have baptized people from my daily prayer list.

1. ....
2. ....
3. ....
4. ....
5. ....

Use these scriptural prayers as a guide to pray regularly for those on your list.

1. Lord, I pray that you draw _____ to Yourself (John 6:44).
2. I pray that _____ will seek to know You (Acts 17:27).
3. I pray that _____ will hear and accept the Word of God for what it really is (1 Thess. 2:13).
4. I ask You, Lord, to prevent Satan from blinding _____ to the truth (2 Cor. 4:4; 2 Tim. 2:25-26).

5. Holy Spirit, I ask You to convict _____ of his/her sin and need for Christ's redemption (John 16:7-14).

6. I ask that You send someone who will share the gospel with _____ (Matt. 9:37-38).

7. I also ask that you give me the opportunity, the courage and the words to share the truth with _____ (Col. 4:3-6; Eph. 6:19-20).

8. Lord, I pray that _____ will turn from his/her sin and follow Christ (Acts 17:30-31; 1 Thess. 1:9-10).

9. Lord, I pray that _____ would put all of his/her trust in Christ (John 1:12, 5:24).

10. Lord, I pray that _____ will confess Christ as Lord, take root and grow in faith and bear much fruit for Your glory (Rom. 10:9-10; Col. 2:6-7; Luke 8:15).[15]

Brothers, my heart's desire and prayer to God for them is that they may be saved.
– ROMANS 10:1

CHAPTER 4

Intimacy and Authority

> In the beginning, God created the heavens and the earth. The earth was without form and void, and darkness was over the face of the deep. And the Spirit of God was hovering over the face of the waters. And God said, "Let there be light," and there was light.
> – GENESIS 1:1-3

Let's take a step back and look at who we are and why we are here. We'll discover the answer to that in the Bible: we were created in God's image, and our purpose is to interact with God in an intimate friendship. God has delegated authority to us, so we can bring His Kingdom to the nations. This divine design becomes clear in the very first chapter of the Bible:

> Then God said, "Let us make man in our image, after our likeness. And let them have dominion over the fish of the sea and over the birds of the heavens and over the livestock and over all the earth and over every creeping thing that creeps on the earth." So God created man in his own image, in the image of God he created him; male and female he created them. And God blessed them. And God said to them, "Be fruitful and multiply and fill the earth and subdue it, and have dominion over the fish

of the sea and over the birds of the heavens and over every living thing that moves on the earth."
— GENESIS 1:26-28

Four principles can be gathered from this passage. The following diagram illustrates these.[16] Let's then go through these one by one.

Invisible aspect	1. Intimacy God wants us to know Him intimately, as His children.	The great commandment Matt. 22:37-40
	2. Transformation Through an intimate relationship with God, we become like Him.	
Visible aspect	3. Authority God delegates His power and authority to us.	The great commission Matt. 28:16-20
	4. Fruitfulness We spread God's Kingdom, His love, healing and power.	

Intimacy

The first principle is intimacy. God wants everyone to know Him intimately as their Father. Genesis 1 reveals that in a general sense, every human is already a child of God because we are all made in His image. We should learn to value people of all kinds of faiths, cultures and political views because everyone reflects something of God's image. Nevertheless, not everyone experiences an intimate relationship with God, because it requires faith in Jesus Christ. That's what the apostle John spoke of when he said:

> To all who did receive him, who believed in his name, he gave the right to become children of God, who were born, not of blood nor of the will of the flesh nor of the will of man, but of God.
> – JOHN 1:12-13

But how can we enter into intimacy with Him? Activities such as self-reflection, prayer, rest, meditation on scripture, study, fasting, silence and solitude can enable us to disconnect with the busy world around us and connect with God. They allow us to cultivate our hearts and create sacred space and time where God can transform us.

Transformation

The second principle is transformation. As we cultivate our relationship with God, we become like Him.

In 2001, I fell in love with a beautiful Dutch woman who radically transformed every aspect of my life. Because I married her, I learned to speak Dutch, eat Gouda cheese every day, and ride a bike with two kids, groceries and a dog. I now live in a wonderful place called Amsterdam. I have four amazing children and a street dog from Romania. I have become a better person by getting to know my wife. Likewise, getting to know God intimately transforms every aspect of our lives. We don't just discover who God is, but in the process we find out who we really are.

So what is the transformation we go through? Through Christ, we are no longer sinners, we are saints (1 Cor. 6:11). We have been made the "righteousness of God" in Christ (2 Cor. 5:21). We are a "chosen people, a royal priesthood, a holy nation". We are God's very own treasured possession (1 Pet. 2:9, NIV). We are loved (Jer. 31:3). We are children of God (1 John 3:1). We are delighted in (Zeph. 3:17). We are forgiven, free and washed clean (1 Pet. 2:24, Gal. 5:1, Isa. 1:18). We are wonderfully made ambassadors of Christ who emit his fragrance everywhere we go (2 Cor. 5:20, 2 Cor. 2:15). We work together with Christ and have a huge inheritance (1 Cor. 3:9, Rom. 8:15-17). Knowing Christ brings us into a new reality.

Henri Nouwen used to say, "You are not what you do. You are not what you have. You are not what people think of you. No, you are a dearly beloved child of God and he is pleased with you."[17] That is a truth I have been able to share on several occasions. As I sat across from people who work in Amsterdam's Red-Light District, I told them, "You are not a sex worker. The real and true identity God wants you to experience is that you are His child and He loves you." As we come into contact with God's love, we are transformed.

Many preachers press their listeners to change their behavior, which may well be necessary, yet often bad behavior is simply a symptom of a deeper problem. Addiction, anger, gambling, depression and sexual immorality often have their root in feeling unloved, full of fear and rejection. These identity issues can be solved by allowing the Gospel to penetrate and heal our heart. Knowing that we are loved, valuable, cared for and safe means that we don't need to anesthetize our pain. God's love gives us permanent satisfaction and freedom.

A friend of mine lived for many years as a homeless criminal and drug addict. He was in and out of jail so often that after being there forty times, he stopped counting. It was in solitary confinement in prison where he was only allowed to read the Bible that he started experiencing God.

As he read the Scriptures, the love of God became very real for him. He began going to church in prison and quit using drugs. He recalls that the first time that he watched the Disney film *Bambi*, he started crying. For so many years, he had tried to cope with his wounded heart by doing drugs and stealing money. Getting to know Christ meant that he got a completely new life. Everything about him was born again! Feelings he had not experienced in decades came flooding back. His conscience and his heart were restored.

It was my joy and honor to baptize him and marry him to his wife. He says Jesus is the greatest person he ever met because through Him everything changed. Before he had thousands of euros, but no peace of mind. Now he has much less money, yet great peace of mind. The Gospel fills our heart and gives us a satisfaction that nothing or nobody can ever take away. Knowing God's love transforms us. We can now love others as He loves us.

Authority

The third principle is that God delegates His power and authority to us. He does so from the very beginning. In Genesis 1, we read that Adam and Eve are given authority over the earth (Gen. 1:28). Tragically, Adam and Eve chose to go against God. They believe Satan rather than God, and thus they give away their authority. Check out what the devil told Jesus when he was tempting Him.

> And the devil took him up and showed him all the kingdoms of the world in a moment of time, and said to him, "To you I will give all this authority and their glory, for it has been delivered to me, and I give it to whom I will. If you, then, will worship me, it will all be yours."
> – LUKE 4:5-7

Jesus did not say, "You're wrong, Satan, you don't have that authority." Nor did He bow down. Jesus accessed the authority and power of another source: His heavenly Father. Satan had no hold on Him (John 14:30). And in His death and resurrection, He enabled us to once again function in our original authority. Interestingly, both God and the devil are limited to how much influence they can have in our lives by our own choices. Jesus longed to care for Jerusalem as a mother hen cares for her chicks, but they "were not willing" (Matt. 23:37). God desired Israel's return to Him so they could live in rest and be safe. They refused (Isa. 30:15). Our daily choices determine whether or not we will live in line with the thoughts and will of God or not.

Before His resurrection, Jesus acted in His Father's authority. He said that He could not do anything by Himself. He only did what He saw his Father doing (John 5:19). His ministry was one of observing where His Father was at work and joining Him. This is a perfect blueprint of how we can also move in God's authority and power.

So how did He know what the Father was doing? Jesus made it a priority to regularly get away from the crowds and spend time alone with his Father. His authority came out of His intimacy with His Father. This is why we must base our lives and power ministry on our intimate time with Father God. This intimacy is available to us, not only during special times of prayer, but all throughout our day. As Graham Cooke says, "The best way to enter the secret place with God is to never leave it."[18]

Jesus did some amazing things. He turned water into wine, walked on water, healed the sick, cast out demons and raised the dead. Even more mind-boggling is that Jesus said we can do all the things that He did and more (John 14:12). Through prayer we can bring heaven to earth and the earth to heaven (Matt. 6:10), just like Jesus did.

Our mandate to do so comes from Jesus Himself:

> All authority in heaven and on earth has been given to me. Go therefore and make disciples of all nations, baptizing them in the name of the Father and of the Son and of the Holy Spirit, teaching them to observe all that I have commanded you. And behold, I am with you always, to the end of the age.
> — MATTHEW 28:18-20

This is the resurrected Jesus speaking. He now has all authority in heaven and on earth. He commissions us to make disciples of all nations by baptizing and teaching them to obey all He has commanded us to do.

We are able to do this because He is literally accompanying, leading and guiding us through the Holy Spirit. He says, "If you abide in me, and my words abide in you, ask whatever you wish, and it will be done for you" (John 15:7).

Fruitfulness

The fourth and final principle is fruitfulness. When we live in intimate friendship with God, are being transformed into His likeness and accept the authority He has given us, we will bear much fruit.

I believe there are heavenly storehouses filled with gifts that God wants to give to men and women. There is salvation. There is healing. There is prophecy. There are words of knowledge. What He needs, however, is people like me and you who will serve as His messengers.

There is a Kingdom to proclaim, and power to accompany that message. What does that entail? Jesus says:

> And proclaim as you go, saying, "The kingdom of heaven is at hand." Heal the sick, raise the dead, cleanse lepers, cast out demons. You received without paying; give without pay.
> – MATTHEW 10:7-8

However, we are to do more than proclaim the Kingdom, we are called to seek it (Matt. 6:33). Dallas Willard says the Kingdom of God "is the range of his effective will, where what he wants is done." It is not adding more religious activities to what we already do, His Kingdom leads us into a personal interactive relationship where He is our constant companion in every area of our lives.[19]

In the Kingdom of God, the thoughts and will of God are experienced and done. Though it is good to use our intellect, the Kingdom of God has heavenly wisdom that cannot be understood with earthly wisdom (John 3:10-12). A key rule in the Kingdom of God is that it is better to give than to receive (Acts 20:35). The best way to lead is to serve and the best way to live is to die (Mark 10:42-45; Matt. 16:25).

Due to the fall of humankind, all of creation has been suffering (Rom. 8:19-21). Creation was placed under the rule of selfishness, greed and darkness. However, when Jesus died and rose again, the Kingdom of God broke into the earth. Every time Jesus healed the sick, cast out demons, fed the multitudes and brought people into connection with Father God, He was demonstrating the Kingdom of God (Matt. 10:7-8; Luke 11:20).

For the time being, there are two competing forces: the powers of darkness and the Kingdom of Light. That's rather like what happened in the Second World War. D-Day, June 6, 1944, was a very real turning point in that war. And yet the war still had to be fought. Now, we all know the outcome of this war, but it could have turned out differently if the allied forces had ceased to fight the Nazis. But they persevered until on May 8, 1945, Nazi forces completely and unconditionally surrendered.

D-Day in the cosmic spiritual battle was when Jesus died and was resurrected. He took back all authority back from Satan and now all rightful authority belongs to Him (Matt. 28:18-20). He has purchased us with His blood and has made us a Kingdom of priests who are to rule the earth (Rev. 5:10). Paul describes this D-Day and its effects like this:

> For if, because of one man's trespass, death reigned through that one man, much more will those who receive the abundance of grace and the free gift of righteousness reign in life through the one man Jesus Christ.
> — ROMANS 5:17

We are called to spread Christ's leadership and dominion everywhere we go. What does that dominion look like? Jesus' leadership style is that of a humble servant. He washed the feet of His disciples. He touched and healed those who were rejected by society. He forgave His enemies and prayed for those who crucified Him. When we spread God's Kingdom, we do so through radical generosity, service, prayer and love.

For the time being, a spiritual war is raging on (Eph. 6:10-12). We experience God's Kingdom breaking through in salvations, healings, signs and wonders, yet there is still sickness, tragedy, brokenness and death. Some people I have prayed for were healed, some were not. I see God's Kingdom break into many lives and situations, yet I also see the darkness wreaking havoc.

The ultimate victory day for the Kingdom of heaven will be when God creates a new heaven and a new earth. The apostle John describes that day with these words:

> No longer will there be anything accursed, but the throne of God and of the Lamb will be in it, and his servants will worship him. They will see his face, and his name will be on their foreheads.
> – REVELATION 22:3-4

Until then, we have a job to do: we reign together with Jesus, bringing His Kingdom, His healing, love, order and power to all of creation.

POWER EVANGELISM — *JUST DO IT!*

Genesis 1:26-28 is a model of how sound and biblical power ministry develops. There is an invisible side to power evangelism that precedes the spectacular things we see. Our authority and power come from our intimate relationship with God. If we neglect this foundation, our power ministry can become dangerous and will not endure.

However, if power ministry is based on the great commandment, this gives it a healthy basis.

QUESTIONS

1. Examine the diagram and discuss the first two points (intimacy and transformation): why is it important to have our identity firmly rooted and grounded in these?

2. Why is it important to live out the great commandment before the great commission?

3. What does it mean to live in the Kingdom of God? How is that different than what most people live?

4. According to Matthew 7:20-23, why is intimacy with Christ crucial in power ministry?

5. To what and where is God calling you to bring His kingdom? How does God's Kingdom manifest (Rom. 14:17; 1 Cor. 4:20)?

CHAPTER 5
How to Heal the Sick

> Heal the sick, raise the dead, cleanse lepers, cast out demons. You received without paying; give without pay.
> — MATTHEW 10:7-8

Every year around my birthday, my mother tells the dramatic and miraculous story of my birth. When my mom went for her checkup toward the end of her pregnancy, the doctors told her, "Your boy is dying. We need to deliver him at once!" The doctors were able to get us into the only hospital with incubators, because they suspected I might need one to survive.

In hospital, my mother was anesthetized for the operation. Unfortunately, the dosage she was given was too high. After I was pulled out of my mother's womb, she stopped breathing. Hospital staff got her breathing again, but instead of watching her, they left her in a hallway all alone!

My mother is a nurse and she knew that she was likely to stop breathing again. The only nurse who came by told her that her baby boy was not expected to live. As she lay there, all she could do was begin to pray, "Even though I walk through the valley of the shadow of death, I will fear no evil, for you are with me" (Ps. 23:4).

She recalls sensing a black cloud coming down. She was fighting for her own life and her baby's. She prayed that God would have other people intercede for her at that moment. She knew that without God's help, we were not going to make it.

Six months later, a friend of hers who lived in Alaska asked my mother what had happened on January 12th. This friend said that on that date she woke up with a sudden urge to pray for us. She had no idea what was going on, but somehow, this woman was made aware that we needed prayer. God used the prayers of a woman in Alaska to save our lives!

The story does not stop there. My parents brought home a very sick child. The doctors later diagnosed me with cerebral palsy and told them I would never walk or talk. Cerebral palsy is incurable. The doctors prepared my parents for what life would look like taking care of a child with CP.

Every day my parents did exercises with my little limbs. My parents loved me and knew that they were going to care for me, no matter what. But they also believed in the power of prayer. They believed that God still does miracles today.

One of the people who was praying for me was my Aunt Candy in California. She had a weekly women's prayer meeting that got together every Thursday. They prayed for me and then did what the apostle Paul did in Acts 19:11-12. They mailed an anointed prayer cloth (actually a tissue) to my mother in Chile. My mother sewed that cloth onto my pajamas. One month later, all effects of cerebral palsy were gone from my little body!

When we returned to the United States six months later, doctors could not tell that I had ever been afflicted with the sickness. It was a miracle, or dare I say, *I am a living miracle!* I know without a doubt that healing is for today, because I have personally experienced it.

Why Pray for Healing?

Praying for the sick is scary. Why should we even bother? The answer is simple; Jesus says, "Heal the sick" (Matt. 10:8, Luke 10:9). Jesus also states, "And these signs will accompany those who believe: in my name ... they will lay their hands on the sick, and they will recover" (Mark 16:17-18). Just as we should give to the poor, pray for our enemies and forgive people, so we should make it a practice of praying for the sick. Healing the sick is a normal part of following Jesus.

But how about those who are not healed when we pray for them? I have been in services where it seemed like nearly everybody I prayed for experienced healing in their bodies. I have also prayed for people without seeing them healed. Not everyone we pray for gets healed, but no one will get healed if we *do not* pray.

What's true for sharing our faith, is also true for praying for healing: not everyone I share my faith with will become a Christian, but that doesn't give me an excuse to keep my mouth shut. Sharing my faith and praying for healing are acts of love. My goal is that no matter what may or may not happen, people know I love them and God loves them. For God, nothing is impossible when we share our faith and pray.

In 2010, I saw several deaf ears pop open. Later that year, I met a deaf man at a park in Amsterdam. I prayed for him, but he was not healed. However, when I finished praying, he did have a tear in his eye and he thanked me for caring enough to pray. Our job is to lovingly pray for healing and leave the results in God's hands.

God heals people, we don't. Relax and pray for healing in a manner that people will feel honored and loved, no matter what. The more you pray for the sick to be healed, the more healings you will see. The more people are praying for the sick, the more people will get healed.

A Prayer Breakthrough

If you want to see a breakthrough in healing, perseverance is essential. That's what Iskander found out. In 2015, this young man joined me on the streets of Amsterdam to pray for people to be healed for the first time. That first day, three people were completely or partially healed after we prayed for them. He was so excited that he joined another friend and started seeing people healed in Amsterdam every day. Eventually, we started going to the streets once a week to pray for strangers.

One week, he told me, "Matt, I am going to pray for people with crutches and believe that they are going to be healed."

The next week, he told me that he had seen his first person with crutches healed. On that same day, we also saw a young Spanish boy healed and able to walk without his crutch anymore.

It was then that he told me, "Matt, now I am going for people in wheelchairs."

The next week, he told me he had seen the first person in a wheelchair healed so that they could stand up and walk. It was awesome!

Then he went to a large Dutch Christian conference to be part of the prayer team to pray for the sick (Opwekking 2016). He stood at the wheelchair section and kept praying for people in wheelchairs. Three of those people were healed that weekend! One of them was Marije de Vries.

One month earlier, Marije had had an operation due to a bone that was sticking out of the side of her foot. Because of the malformation of her foot, she had had pain in her back and hips throughout her life. She had had to wait for this operation until her feet had finished growing. The doctors cut and pasted different bones and tendons to her foot so that she would be able to walk normally. The recovery time was supposed to be at least three months, and she would be in pain for at least a year.

Now, she was attending the conference. Along with others, Iskander repeatedly prayed for her Friday, Saturday, and Sunday. However, instead of the pain decreasing, it increased. And then she even slipped and fell on her foot. However, she was determined to not stop praying for her complete healing.

On Monday, she refused to go home before she was prayed for again. She found Iskander and another young man and asked them to pray for her once more. The two prayed for her repeatedly until the healing started taking place.[20] Marije went from having severe and constant pain to being able to run while pushing her wheelchair without any pain!

Marije had to wait two weeks before her cast could be removed. The doctors were astounded by what they found. Her foot was completely healed and she was free to do whatever she wanted!

If Marije had given up after receiving prayer on Friday, Saturday and Sunday, she might not have been healed on Monday. Don't give up when you pray for healing!

Persevering

A prime example of such perseverance in prayer can be found in John Wimber's story.[21] Wimber felt God called him to pray for the sick at his church in Anaheim, California. For ten months, Wimber and his team prayed, but not a single person got healed after receiving prayer. In fact, the people praying for healing were getting sick themselves after praying for others. Wimber wanted to stop, but God did not let him. After nine months of faithfully praying for healing, he saw the first person healed. That was the beginning of a healing ministry that helped launch the Vineyard movement. His ministry affected many other denominations and movements around the world.

Wimber's experience is not unique. After Todd White[22] was dramatically delivered from a life of crime and drug addiction, he discovered divine healing. For three and a half months he prayed for ten people a day to be healed. He prayed at supermarkets. He prayed at gas stations. He prayed at work. Everywhere he went, he would pray for people to be healed. After having prayed for more than nine hundred people for healing, he finally saw the first healing take place. Now White is seeing healings every day as God gives him words of knowledge everywhere he goes.

Jordan Seng describes his struggle with healing ministry in his book *Miracle Work*.

> If you believe God enables you to perform supernatural feats, you'll sometimes feel terrible when you fail. At our church's healing services, roughly half of those who come for ministry receive at least partial physical healing during the service. Many experience progressive healing afterward, and about 15 percent receive total and immediate healing during the service itself. We register about a 10 percent success rate even with ostensibly incurable diseases. We seem to have an almost perfect success rate with some diseases, and our breakthrough rate for deliverance ministry is also quite high. We're in no way approaching Jesus' level of power and effectiveness, but I guess you could say there's cause for encouragement. Yet when we fail to heal a beautiful little girl with leukemia or a young mom with brain tumors, we feel the bite, and almost always wonder if we should have done better.[23]

I grew up watching my father, Dean, pray for thousands of people who were healed of many kinds of sicknesses. He wrote to me about some of the joys, but also frustrations, of praying for the sick. Here are some of the experiences he shared:

> In a service in Tomé (Chile), I prayed five successive nights for a fifteen-year-old with no hip socket who limped badly. As he limped away from the prayer line that last night of services, I felt like crawling down a hole! I had prayed my best and my hardest and nothing had happened.
>
> I decided to hide my feelings of disappointment and continue praying for the sick, but without testing the rest to see if they were healed. A lady brought up her little eighteen-month-old boy for prayer. I asked her what his problem was, and she said that he had the same problem as that fifteen-year-old: no hip socket from birth. My faith for this healing was very low.
>
> A few minutes later, the congregation started cheering. I learned that the little boy had gotten a new hip socket when I prayed for him and was walking down the aisle and with no limp at all! Many of his relatives came to faith because of this healing.
>
> Still, I was disturbed. Why did God heal him and not the fifteen-year-old?
>
> Finally I had enough! I told the Lord that I was through praying for the sick. I would preach the Gospel so that people would get saved, but I just couldn't take all of the embarrassing failures when I prayed for them! I would even stop fasting and praying before the meetings!
>
> The next meeting I preached, people came up to give to their lives to the Lord, and I sat down, smugly thinking I was done. But the pastor got

up and announced to the congregation: "Brother Dean is now going to pray for the sick!"

Boy, was I mad! I told the Lord, "No. You can't do this to me! I can't take being disappointed again by praying for severe cases and not seeing them healed."

However, I didn't want to embarrass the pastor, so I got up and started laying hands on the people one-by-one.

Amazing healings started taking place. A girl who had not been able to lift up her right arm could now lift it above her head. A girl with a blind eye could suddenly see perfectly. More healings took place, and I had not even prayed and fasted before the service!

After the service, I repented. I told the Lord that no matter how embarrassed I got, I would keep on praying for the sick. I would obey His commandment to heal the sick, no matter how weak my faith might be or disappointed I could feel. I have never regretted that decision!

What to Do

The Bible mentions many ways of going about healing. Some of these include: laying on hands (Luke 4:40); casting out demons (Matt. 8:16); breaking a curse (Gal. 3:13-14); using anointing oil (Mark 6:13); speaking out in faith (Mark 11:23); touching clothes or objects (Mark 5:27-30; Acts 19:12; 2 Kings 13:21); fasting (Isa. 58:5-8); and speaking God's Word (Ps. 107:20).

Though there are many ways to heal the sick, you might find it helpful to follow a simple model. My brother Aaron was once asked to train Brazilian teenagers to pray for the sick.

He came up with these five steps to pray for healing, and has seen thousands of healings as a result.

1. When appropriate, place your hands on the area(s) of sickness
There is biblical precedent for this. Jesus says, "they will lay their hands on the sick, and they will recover" (Mark 16:18).

When praying for the sick, always ask for permission before you lay your hands on a person. If it is inappropriate to place your hand where they are sick, place your hand on their head or shoulder. Never push someone or place your weight on them! If it is inappropriate to lay a hand on someone, but they allow you to pray, do it. It is not about following a model but giving space to God to do a miracle.

2. Command the body part to be healed – In Matthew 8:3, we read, "Jesus reached out and touched him. 'I am willing,' he said. 'Be healed!' And instantly the leprosy disappeared" (NLT).

Jesus never asked the Father to heal the sick. He always commanded the sick to be healed. Jesus has all authority, and He has given this authority to us (see Matt. 28:18-20; John 14:12-14; Matt. 10:1). The prayer for healing He shows us is not a request but a command based on the spiritual authority He has given to us.

3. Command any spirits of sickness to leave – Some sicknesses (not all) are caused by demons. In Luke 13:10-13, we read about Jesus healing a woman who had suffered from a disabling spirit for eighteen years. It is useful to pray, "If there is any spirit of sickness present, I command you to leave in the name of Jesus."

A possible sign of demonic activity is when the pain in their body starts moving around when you command it to leave. If you discern spiritual activity, don't stop praying until you feel this has subsided, and do not be intimidated.

4. Ask them to try what they could not do – In the Bible, we read:

> On another Sabbath, he entered the synagogue and was teaching, and a man was there whose right hand was withered ... And after looking around at them all he said to him, "Stretch out your hand." And he did so, and his hand was restored.
> – LUKE 6:6,10

At times, a person does not realize they are healed until they start testing themselves. This means if a person suffers from back pain or neck pain, I will ask them to bend over or look to their right and left. Make sure they don't hurt themselves doing this, but don't skip this step. Often this act of faith *releases* healing. My father prayed once for a man whose foot was bent completely to the left. He told him to try to kick his foot, and the third time he kicked, his foot straightened out!

Another example. Marlene Klepees suffered from cerebral palsy (the same disease I was born with). During prayer one day she had a vision of Jesus telling her she was going to be healed. She called a local church and asked them to pray for her.

The pastor prayed for her and then asked her, "Would you be willing to get out of the wheelchair, by faith?" She got up and started running around the church. She was completely healed. Getting out of the wheelchair was the step of faith God used to heal her.[24]

It is vital that people get themselves checked out by a doctor. If they are on medications, they should not cease immediately. If they are healed, the doctor will be able to verify this. Just as Jesus sent the lepers to the temple to be checked if they were cleansed, so we should have ourselves checked out. Having doctors verify and document healings is a great way to testify that Jesus still heals today.

5. Evaluate results, and if necessary, repeat steps 1-4 – Jesus had to pray for a blind man twice before he was totally healed (see Mark 8:23-25). If Jesus had to pray twice, you and I may need to pray twenty times. If a person is not completely healed after praying once, keep on praying! As long as the person is engaged and you find it appropriate, keep praying.

One woman who attended our church was healed of fibromyalgia after praying for her for more than three years. Every time we prayed for her, she felt a little better. And then, one day she forgave someone and was completely healed after we prayed. Healing is often a process, so do not give up after praying once.

Have the courage to ask a person, "So how are you feeling now?" Rate their pain on a scale of 0-10 (10 being the level of pain they had before you began praying and 0 being pain-free).

Celebrate every time the pain has decreased on the scale, and keep praying believing for a zero.

Also, you don't need to pray long and with many words. When praying for strangers on the street, I pray short prayers so that I can pray two or three times. It is not the length of your prayer that creates the miracle.

In Bunschoten, the Netherlands, I shared these five steps to pray for healing during a Sunday morning service. There was a man with chronic stomach aches. A friend prayed for him no less than eight times before the aches disappeared. He has not suffered from that pain since. It was fortunate that his friend did not stop praying after the seventh time.

Questions About Healing

Healing is a hotly debated issue. I'll go through three key questions it raises.

Do people have to have faith to be healed? The short answer is no. In Europe, relatively few people believe in God, and yet I see quite a few healings on the streets when I pray for unbelievers. Our job is simply to pray and believe and trust God, no matter what. We should never say people do not have enough faith if they do not get healed. That does not help them at all. Instead, make it your goal that whether or not they get healed, they will feel that you cared enough to pray for them.

Does my faith have to be high to heal the sick? Again, the short answer is no. John Wimber told this story to illustrate that people's healings do not depend on us:

> I remember standing at a urinal in an airport in Phoenix. A guy leaned over and put his face in front of mine and said, "You're him, aren't you?"
> He wanted to shake hands with me. I said, "I'm a little busy right now."
> He said, "Will you pray for me?"
> I said, "Before or after I wash my hands?" This actually happened! I could not believe it! So I washed my hands and prayed for him. I heard through a friend of his that he was healed ... Right at that moment all I had was anger. I never felt so put off in my life! It certainly wasn't my faith, but I did do what Jesus commissioned me to do.[25]

What about the people who don't get healed? I am always amazed how people who don't believe in God or healing get healed when I pray for them. I am also amazed when people who are full of faith and believe in God do not get healed themselves.

The first time we did power evangelism on the street, we did not see any healings take place until after four hours of standing there. Then, one woman asked us to pray for her back and neck pain and it immediately disappeared. Suddenly in a timespan of five minutes we saw four more people get healed as others asked for prayer. Perhaps, then, people aren't healed because they simply do not ask (James 4:2-3). How many people walked by our tent that day who could have been healed but were not because they did not ask?

There can be obstacles for people being healed. These may include: unforgiveness, spiritual oppression, fear, a curse, etc. In his hometown, Jesus was limited because of people's unbelief. It says, "he could do no mighty work ... except that he laid his hands on a few sick people and healed them" (Mark 6:5).

The healing ministry is also a reminder of the cosmic spiritual battle going on around us. Jesus came "to destroy the works of the devil" and sickness is a work of the darkness (1 John 3:8). This is why we pray for healing.

It is not generally a person's fault that they are sick. It is part of the brokenness of this world. There are many poignant stories of healing evangelists dying of sicknesses. John Wimber saw many people healed in his ministry, yet he himself had serious recurring health problems. He was sixty-three when he died from a stroke after a fall. Billy Joe Daugherty, founding pastor of Victory Christian Center in Tulsa, Oklahoma, saw countless healings. He passed away from cancer. Can I explain why one person gets healed and the other does not? No, I can't. Fortunately, I don't have to.

I am not God, and I cannot heal anyone in my own strength. God heals, I don't. But what I can do, is relax and pray for healing in such a way that no matter what happens, people will have experienced God's love through me.

For years I coached my son and daughter's soccer team. One of my instructions is that when they are near the opponent's goal, they should shoot. They do not score every time they shoot, but they cannot score if they don't shoot. It is the same with praying for the sick, prophesying, and sharing our faith with unbelievers—if we do not do it, nothing can happen and we are withholding something precious. Because how can they hear unless we speak? How can they be healed unless we pray? The apostle Paul eloquently writes:

> How then will they call on him in whom they have not believed? And how are they to believe in him of whom they have never heard? And how are they to hear without someone preaching?
> ROMANS 10:14

Let's reach out to people so they can be experience God's healing and saving touch through our touch!

POWER EVANGELISM—*JUST DO IT!*

EXERCISE 1
Pray for the sick
Think of people you know who need healing and then go pray for their healing. Use the five steps and see what happens. Set a goal. For example, aim at praying for ten people in the two weeks or months or two people next time you go to church.

EXERCISE 2
Praying for healing from a distance
Pray for someone on the phone or send a prayer cloth to someone far away who needs healing (Acts 19:12).

EXERCISE 3
Have a healing service
Plan a special meeting or Bible study to talk about healing and then practice praying for healing for one another.

CHAPTER 6
How to Use Words of Knowledge

> But if all of you are prophesying, and unbelievers or people who don't understand these things come into your meeting, they will be convicted of sin and judged by what you say. As they listen, their secret thoughts will be exposed, and they will fall to their knees and worship God, declaring, "God is truly here among you."
> — 1 CORINTHIANS 14:24-25 (NLT)

A powerful way of drawing people's attention to God is through words of knowledge. Just so we're on the same page here, what are words of knowledge? David Betts gives a great definition:

> A word of knowledge is a supernatural revelation about a fact about a person or a situation that does not come from human thoughts, but from the Spirit of God. It is one of the revelatory gifts which include words of knowledge, wisdom, prophecy and discernment.[26]

An example of how that might work: one day on the street, I asked a man whether I could tell him what I saw in him. I then told him that I saw him driving a forklift truck. That turned out to be what he did for a living. I had his attention when I began sharing more about Jesus and the Gospel.

Graham Cooke gives a helpful analysis of the purpose of words of knowledge. He says, "Prophecy is made up of three elements: word of knowledge, gift of prophecy, and word of wisdom. A word of knowledge opens up the issue, a prophetic word speaks God's heart into it, and a word of wisdom tells us how to respond to God."[27]

The terminology "word of knowledge" might not be familiar to you, but if you look at Jesus' ministry here on earth, you'll recognize what it is.

Jesus' Words of Knowledge

In the Bible, we read many examples of Jesus giving words of knowledge. Let's take a closer look.

Often, Jesus gives words of knowledge for the instruction of His disciples. One well-known example is when He gives a very precise description on how to prepare for His entry into Jerusalem:

> Go into the village in front of you, and immediately you will find a donkey tied, and a colt with her. Untie them and bring them to me. If anyone says anything to you, you shall say, "The Lord needs them," and he will send them at once.
> – MATTHEW 21:2-3

And that's just what happens! Another example: on one occasion, He tells Peter to go fishing and pull a coin out of the first fish he catches (see Matt. 17:27).

Jesus also gives words of knowledge that sound more general—if we gave them, we might be uncertain of their value. But these words, too, have the power to transform lives. That's what happens in Nathanael's case. When Philip tells Nathanael about Jesus, Nathanael's response is cynicism and unbelief. "Can anything good come out of Nazareth?" (John 1:46). Jesus gives two words of knowledge. One describes Nathanael: "Behold, an Israelite indeed, in whom there is no deceit!" (John 1:47). The other is about where he was sitting when he heard about Jesus: "Before Philip called you, when you were under the fig tree, I saw you" (John 1:48). Such simple words transform Nathanael's life and cause him to open up to Jesus.

And then there is the story of Jesus' conversation with a Samaritan woman at a well. During the conversation, Jesus shares a word of knowledge:

> You have had five husbands, and the one you now have is not your husband.
> — JOHN 4:18

Jesus does not use this information to put her down. Instead, He speaks into her potential of becoming a true worshiper. As a response, she runs back to her village and tells her friends, "Come, see a man who told me all that I ever did. Can this be the Christ?" (John 4:29). Talk about a life-changing word of knowledge!

Evangelism with Words of Knowledge

If Jesus used words of knowledge in His ministry, so can we. In fact, I regularly use them when I do power evangelism. Instead of beginning a conversation by talking about Jesus, I ask people if I can tell them what I see in them. If they say yes, I ask God for a word of knowledge and go for it. Sometimes I say something that is just plain wrong, but often people do say, "How did you know that?" This opens opportunities to talk about Jesus with people who otherwise would not be interested in talking about Him at all.

An example. One day, I took a group of Bible school students to a shopping center in Amersfoort, the Netherlands. As we drove there, we asked God for words of knowledge. Three words popped up: a bread bakery, Mary and back pain.

After ten minutes of walking around, two excited students came to me saying, "We went to the bread bakery and there was a lady called Mary outside. She had back pain. We prayed for her, and the pain disappeared." Using accurate words of knowledge to share Jesus' love and power with people is such fun!

Another example: I sometimes go to psychic fairs in order to minister to everyone who comes to my table using the gifts of the Holy Spirit. I have seen Jesus heal and speak to many people at such places. At one psychic fair near Amsterdam, two people sat down at my table. I proceeded to tell one of them about their work and the things that had happened in the recent past and the things that needed to be done in the next six months. I described her role and responsibility. The words of knowledge kept flowing, and I was astounded at the level of details and information I was giving her.

A little later, she told me that everything I said was true and that she was absolutely amazed. I was so excited that I got to use words of knowledge to show that Jesus is real and that He cares for her and her work. Words of knowledge show people that God is real. They help them trust that God can come through for them.

One man who came to a meeting I was prophesying at was shocked when I told him, "Your wife loves you very, very much!" What I did not know is that he had just had an argument with his wife and had left the house saying, "Do you still love me?" God let him know that his wife loved him very much even though they had just had an argument.

Getting Words of Knowledge

So how can we get words of knowledge? Putty Putman explains, "Getting a word of knowledge is often a very subtle matter; more often than not, we think that it is us instead of God. Stepping out in risk is the only way we will find out if we are hearing God correctly."[28]

There are many ways to get a word of knowledge, but they often come in through our five senses: seeing, feeling, hearing, speaking and smelling. Let's look at each of them.

Seeing – We might receive a dream or a vision in our mind's eye. These pictures or words may be superimposed upon people or things.

For example, I once attended a prayer meeting in London when a woman walked up to me and said, "I see the word discouragement on your head, but God has wiped that away." Her words were accurate. I had just gone through a difficult time, but I was entering a new phase, and I was full of hope.

The pictures God shows us may be literal or symbolic, which means we will often have to interpret them. However, we will not know whether they are literal or symbolic unless we share them.

For example, I have seen mental pictures of someone running over a hurdle, dancing, delivering a baby, working on an oil rig or driving a forklift. Later, I found out this was literally what they did in life. Other times I saw a mental picture of a Santa Clause or a certain animal and I knew they were figurative words and not literal.

During worship, my brother will often see a mental picture of different body parts that God is about to heal. Once he starts ministering, he describes what he saw, and many people are healed through those words of knowledge.

My mother once saw a vision while praying that their landlord would ask them to move out of their house. The next week, everything took place just as she had seen it. God can prepare us for events through daytime visions and night-time dreams.

At times, we may also see or experience the presence of God, angels or demons. This is part of the gift of discernment of spirits. I have occasionally felt the manifest presence of God and angels. These moments are often followed by a wave of God's presence, in which healings or supernatural things may take place. I have also felt an evil spirit enter a room. When that happens, I know how to pray and be alert. At times, I have been told that an evil presence I felt coming into the building is a real issue that people there are dealing with. I nearly always speak of God's presence when I experience it, but I don't generally publicly give any attention to any evil spirit I may be sensing. We should not be surprised to encounter the Holy Spirit, angels or demonic spirits. After all, Jesus Himself and biblical believers experienced the same.

Feeling – If you get a pain or emotion that does not seem to belong to you, that might be a word of knowledge. I was in Eastern Europe once when a woman on my team told me, "I am getting really afraid suddenly. Look, I am literally shaking." I told her, "Relax. It is a word of knowledge. You are picking up a strong spirit of fear in this region."

A prophet on my ministry team was at one of our meetings when she started struggling with thoughts of doubts and cynicism. She thought, "This prophecy stuff is all false. None of this is real." She recognized that these were not her own thoughts. She looked next to her, and there were about six people with their arms crossed refusing to do any of the activations. She started prophesying over them, and they started opening up. She realized that she had actually picked up their thoughts.

With regard to the ministry of healing, if you suddenly feel pain somewhere, it could be a word of knowledge that God wants to heal someone of that condition. Feel free to ask, "Does someone have pain here?" If someone does, pray—and do not be surprised when they get healed!

Hearing – I have never heard the audible voice of God with my physical ears, but I have heard Him speak loudly in my heart. There are times when He has given me names of places to which I would travel and minister. Normally, I just keep that information to myself and see when, how and if it would come to pass.

One Sunday I woke up with a name in my mind. Nobody at the church I visited that Sunday had that name. Later that week, I was in England and prophesied over a pastor—that God would use him mightily in Italy. I then found out that he had just been in Italy and he had been ministering to a pastor who lived in a city with the same name that I had woken up thinking about earlier that week.

Another example. Before I decided to get involved in ministry to prostitutes, I was praying when suddenly I heard loud words in my spirit, *"Set my people free!"* I felt God was speaking and confirming His desire that we help people find true freedom.

Speaking – My mother once received a cake from our neighbors in Chile. As she started to cut it, she heard herself say, "There is glass inside of the cake." Sure enough, she cut open the cake and found pieces of glass inside of it. The neighbors had broken a bottle of milk accidentally and pieces of the glass had ended up in the cake batter. That "automatic speaking," where something just popped out of her mouth, may have saved someone's life.

Sometimes while prophesying I will say things such as, "There are three things that are important in your life right now." Then I pray, "God what are those three things?" As I speak, I hear myself say those three things I did not know.

Smelling – This has not happened to me yet, but many of my friends can actually smell the presence of God and demons. They can smell things in the Spirit. One prophet was doing a deliverance service, when she told her husband to quit passing gas. He said, "I am not passing gas." She was actually smelling evil spirits.

Delivering Words of Knowledge

Words of knowledge[29] can be simply a quick flash of a thought or feeling that can easily be explained away as something you are making up. Anyone can get a word of knowledge, and that is why it is important to become aware that what we are experiencing *could* be a word of knowledge.

So if you think you might have received a word of knowledge, what do you do with it? Firstly, offer words of knowledge, but do not impose them on people. I once heard someone say they walked up to a pregnant woman and said, "It is going to be a boy, and you have to name him Jeremiah." That person went over the woman's boundaries. No one can force someone else to do something they don't want to through a word of knowledge. That person could have offered her a suggestion, "Hey, if it is a boy, how about naming him Jeremiah?"

Secondly, do not necessarily say all that you see. For example, if you see sin in someone's life, do not begin to tell them all their sins, weaknesses and failures. Instead ask God how to best address them and learn to prophesy the better things God has for them.

Graham Cooke was once ministering to a group of leaders when he saw a vision of one of the leaders with a huge knife. God showed him that he was a jealous man who was slandering the head leader. Cooke did not say what he saw. Instead, he delivered a message which changed both of those leaders' lives. He had the jealous leader stand back to back with the head leader. Then he told him, "God calls you to watch and cover his back. You two will be great friends and God will use your ministries to impact only this church, but many churches." The man started weeping like a baby.

Graham Cooke did not dishonor this man for what he was doing, but instead, began speaking about his potential and what God was calling him to do. Twenty years after that prophetic word, the two men are close friends and what he prophesied has come to pass.[30] How you deliver a word is just as important as the word itself.

Know that you may be wrong, but don't worry about it if you are! Just make sure you deliver it in a way that is gracious and humble. Many times, I will give a word of knowledge and no one will respond until after the service or days later, saying that they were the person I was describing.

If you would like to prophesy, but don't know how to start, you could use a springboard such as: "People have said to you that _____." "You have said _____," or "When you were ____ years old _____." This is a step of faith where you simply say whatever comes to you after you have started the springboard.

Please get feedback. If you were right, then you know it was the Holy Spirit. If you were wrong, you can also learn from that. Learning from mistakes will help your become a better prophetic minister.

And my final tip: just do it! During a School of Prophecy in Amsterdam, a leader from my church was prophesying over different individuals, encouraging, strengthening and comforting people. I was aware, though, that if she took some risks, she could get more revelation about these people's past, present and future. I told her, "Go ahead and tell people things about themselves: what they have said, what has taken place, or what may take place in their lives." She went for it. She looked at me and said, "I see you on the airplane from Ukraine and there is a woman with red pants and grey hair sitting next to you." Afterwards she asked, *"Will you please let me know if it really happens?*" As I was flying back from the Ukraine, I looked across the aisle from me and there was the woman with red pants and grey hair. That word of knowledge was spot on. Sadly, this lady was asleep all throughout the journey, and I was unable to engage her in conversation.

Words of Knowledge for Groups

Words of knowledge aren't just for individuals; groups can receive them, too. In Acts 13, we read about the church of Antioch, a church full of prophets and teachers who ask God for knowledge regarding what He wants them to do next. They pray and fast, and the Holy Spirit speaks clearly to them:

> While they were worshiping the Lord and fasting, the Holy Spirit said, "Set apart for me Barnabas and Saul for the work to which I have called them." Then after fasting and praying they laid their hands on them and sent them off.
> – ACTS 13:2-3

A word of knowledge giving to a group also deeply impacted my father's life. In 1967, he was a student at Oral Roberts University. Some time that year, the school had chosen to take three students to Chile for special meetings, and my father explains how the decision was made who should go.

> A friend of mine happened to overhear the seminary professors speaking in the hallway. Their discussion went something like this: "How in the

world are we going to pick just three of the seminary students to go to Chile? Couldn't we just send all sixty?"

This friend could not hold back from speaking up. He said, "You are all Spirit-filled men of God. You all have your doctorates in theology, don't you? Why don't you just ask God who He wants to send?"

His words hit home. They went into an empty classroom, knelt down, and asked God to reveal to them which three seminary students were to go. Then they each wrote down three names that came to them. When they compared the names, they were all the same! God had answered their prayer.

And that is how I was selected to go to Chile in April of 1967, never suspecting that I would eventually spend fifteen years of my life there with my family, working with the national Pentecostal churches.[31]

The prayers of those professors led to a decision that would change my father's life, and my life as well.

Growing in Words of Knowledge

We can expect God to speak to us because it is His pleasure to reveal things to us (see Eph. 1:9). So when I go and evangelize on the street, I often ask God for some information ahead of time. Sometimes nothing that I write down takes place but often it does.

When taking a team to the streets in Fresno, we realized that about half the things we had written down took place. We decided we wouldn't mourn what did not happen, but celebrate what did. Part of growing in words of knowledge is taking risks. You will never grow in words of knowledge if you are afraid of being wrong. Shawn Bolz is a well-known prophet who often gets very accurate words of knowledge. When he ministers, he often shares words of knowledge about names, addresses, birth dates, telephone numbers, (parts of) bank account numbers of people he has never met. He describes his journey in growing in words of knowledge as pretty much trial and error. He recalls how when living in Kansas City he would be in a car with friends and try to get words of knowledge for people these friends knew, and not get anything right. However, God honored his hunger, and he eventually started getting accurate words of knowledge.[32] I enjoy watching him give words of knowledge because he does it with great humility. He recognizes that he is taking a risk and regularly gets a word wrong.

Don't fear getting a word of knowledge wrong, but keep stepping out by faith because you don't know what a word of knowledge can do. Sometimes, it takes time before a word of knowledge "materializes." In November 2016, I gave several words of knowledge in a church in Kiev. I asked if there was anyone who had had a car accident in 2013 and was suffering from back pain. No one responded in a church with more than one thousand people present. In May 2017, I was back in Kiev teaching on words of knowledge at a youth camp. A member of my ministry team saw random numbers and he did not know what they meant. It turned out the numbers corresponded to the license plate of a man who had had a car accident in 2013. His back had been healed earlier that morning during the session on divine healing.

So don't worry if no one responds to your words of knowledge. It may just be a matter of time. There was a six-month time lag between giving that word of knowledge and meeting the man who had had the car accident in 2013.

It may also be that people are afraid to come forward. I was speaking at a youth group once when I got a pain in my wrist, which was a word of knowledge. A woman came forward with pain in her wrist. She was healed after I prayed for her. Then I got pain right in the middle of my back between my shoulder blades. I asked if anyone had pain there and nobody responded. What I did not know was that the same woman whose wrist was healed had a sister-in-law with pain in that exact spot. However, she did not dare come forward to ask prayer for her sister-in-law who was not present. The next day she told her sister-in-law about the word of knowledge, and at that moment, she was healed! They thought that I must have prayed for her or done something special. In reality, all I had said was, "Does anyone have pain right here in your back?" That word of knowledge released faith for her to be healed. Accurate words of knowledge release faith in people's hearts and show them that God is real and that He loves them. They can challenge people to do things they never thought of doing. So step out, just do it!

POWER EVANGELISM—*JUST DO IT!*

EXERCISE 1
Restaurant evangelism
Ask God for a word of knowledge for your waiter at a restaurant. Write down something about them on a napkin and then casually ask about what you have written down. If it is accurate, that may be an opportunity to share more.

EXERCISE 2
Street evangelism
Ask God who or what you are going to see when you go to the street to do power evangelism. Make a list beforehand and when you return, share what you saw and experienced. Don't be surprised if things turn out differently than you thought.

EXERCISE 3
Healing meeting
When conducting a healing meeting, ask God to give you words of knowledge for healing. Write down the healings you feel God may be speaking about and then ask if people are present with those conditions. Pray for their healing.

CHAPTER 7

How to Grow in Power Evangelism

> I will not venture to speak of anything except what Christ has accomplished through me to bring the Gentiles to obedience—by word and deed, by the power of signs and wonders, by the power of the Spirit of God—so that from Jerusalem and all the way around to Illyricum I have fulfilled the ministry of the gospel of Christ ...
> — ROMANS 15:18-19

It is very scary to walk up to a complete stranger and offer to pray for their healing or to give an encouraging word for them. What are they going to say? Are they going to think you are crazy? Maybe they will experience God. Or maybe they'll think you should be locked up. But if you want to grow in power evangelism, you have to step out. Just do it! This requires taking risks. As Wimber always said, *"Faith is spelled R-I-S-K."*

Power evangelism breaks down barriers. People who want to hear nothing about Jesus suddenly have a change of heart after they are healed or receive an accurate word of knowledge. Plenty of reason to go for it!

I've had wonderful results with power evangelism. Whenever I give a presentation at a psychic fair, I do not use any Christian terminology because some people are hostile to the Church and to Christianity. I simply title my lecture, "Demonstrations of the Supernatural Power of Love." I tell testimonies of people being healed by my "Source" (Jesus Christ). Then I tell everyone that my source is going to heal people there. As soon as people see these healings, I offer to reveal my source: Jesus Christ. People are then open to hearing more about Him and His message, because they have seen evidence of His healing power.

After sharing the Gospel, I will ask who would like to receive a personal word from Jesus Christ. Normally *everyone* present does. People are often amazed and confused because they did not know Jesus Christ has authority and spiritual power.

Once I went to downtown Amsterdam to practice power evangelism. The first thirty minutes, no one accepted my offer of prayer. Then we saw a group of high school kids on a school trip who were goofing around. We talked to them and were allowed to pray for one of them. As soon as he experienced healing in his knee, more of the students started asking us to pray for them. When we told one of them what we saw in him, others were also eager to hear what we saw in them. In a matter of five minutes, we saw about five healings take place. We got to talk and pray for an entire group of students!

One of the students' fathers came to us afterwards and told us his son was healed and that we truly had awesome gifts. We got to share more about Jesus and were able to pray for him and other students before they had to get on the bus and leave.

What About Gifting?

You may think, "Yeah, but I don't have the gift of evangelism, healing, prophecy, or words of knowledge." Or, "I am not holy enough to use these gifts." However, all of these gifts, like our salvation, come by grace through faith and not because we work hard or deserve them (Eph. 2:8-9). God is generous. He wants to give us more than we can imagine. I believe these gifts are available for all believers. If you want to grow in power evangelism, the Bible has good advice for you: 'Pursue love, and earnestly desire the spiritual gifts, especially that you may prophesy' (1 Cor. 14:1). (For more on developing the gift of prophecy, check out my book *Prophesy—Just Do It!*)

I have grown in the spiritual gifts by studying them and seeking out those who are strong in them. I ask God for these gifts for myself and have seen Him grant me my request. I hang out with people who are further along than myself. I regularly minister with teams with individuals who have strong spiritual gifting I don't necessarily have (yet). When working together, everyone grows, and team ministry is generally more dynamic and fun than going it alone.

I look for people who are more experienced than I am, and I look for people who want to learn from me. Both groups help me grow. However, always look for those who use their gifts in love and who are committed to building sincere and healthy relationships.

Power Evangelism is for Everybody

There is a danger in using examples like John Wimber, Todd White and myself as power evangelists. We are all extraverts and people who do not fear talking to strangers and doing "crazy" things. Power evangelism is not only for extraverts, though. Power evangelism is sharing the Gospel in a normal and natural way in your daily life. If you can love people and pray for them, power evangelism is for you.

Many of my friends practice power evangelism in their own, more introverted way. The pastor of our Dutch church in Amsterdam has set up a free soup kitchen in our neighborhood. Over the course of a free meal in a relaxed conversation, faith is shared and prayers are prayed. Another friend of mine who is very prophetic is an engineer with a doctorate in chemistry. At his secular workplace, he prophesies over two to three people a week. He does not necessarily use Christian vocabulary, but he shares a message from God with his co-workers.

Another introverted friend of mine simply made the decision that if she heard someone share they had pain or were sick, she would try to ask whether she could pray for them. Power evangelism is not only for certain personality types or "super-Christians." It is for everyone.

As we have seen, Jesus did what He saw his father doing (John 5:19). He knew what His Father was doing, and joined Him. We can do the same. Evangelism is easier when we don't just force ourselves to go talk to strangers all the time, but when we ask God to lead us.

One day I went to a park with a friend. I really wanted to pray for a stranger and share the Gospel. However, I did not feel it was the moment to approach a stranger. As I began praying for my friend, a stranger approached us and asked us to pray for him. In a park with thousands of people, we happened to sit next to someone curious and desiring to know more about God.

In Acts 14:9, Paul sees a crippled man with faith to be healed. This implies that Paul notices something in that man. There was an opening Paul detects that leads to a significant public healing. Not only that man, but many people heard the Gospel preached through this miracle.

So how do we step out in power evangelism? Simple; we say what we feel the Father is saying and we do what we feel He is doing. Even the most introverted believer can do this. Power evangelism can be done by people with all different types of personalities!

Spiritual Disciplines

Spiritual disciplines such as fasting, prayer and sacrificial giving are great catalysts for growing in power evangelism. After all, God's presence brings power with it. Entire days of prayer and fasting where I spent hours prophesying and praying for individuals has definitely sped up development and accuracy of spiritual gifts. If you don't see healings take place immediately, keep praying and believe that breakthrough will come. We do not *earn* spiritual power, but we do position ourselves to receive it from God.

Seek God and He will reward you. Know, however, that God healing people through your prayers is not dependent on how good or godly you are. Peter told the crowd who began to worship him after a lame beggar was healed, "Men of Israel, why do you wonder at this, or why do you stare at us, as though by our own power or piety we have made him walk?" (Acts 3:12).

The famous power evangelist T.L. Osborn was once asked, "What kind of price do you have to pay to have a healing ministry?" Many may think that you have to go pray and fast in a cave for forty days before God can use you. However, Osborn responded by saying, "There is a high price that must be paid to be in the healing ministry, but fortunately Jesus paid the price fully on the cross."[33] It is not what we have to do to deserve God's power, but what Jesus has done for us on the cross.

The Growth Process

Here is a helpful chart to how the process of growing in power evangelism can look like.[34] It can be used by both individuals and groups.

Power Evangelism Growth Process	
1. Base your identity on the Gospel	This is the bedrock for practicing power evangelism; everything feeds back into who you are in Christ.
2. Activate your spiritual gifts	Take part in a school of prophecy.[35]

3. Practice in created spaces	This could be a small group or a Holy Spirit night in your church.
4. Practice outside created spaces	Give prophetic words to people anywhere and anytime. Start praying for healing for people who have not asked for prayer.
5. Use your eyes outside of your church	Start with praying for healing for conditions you can see. Work your way up in risk. Ask for feedback and find out if they are healed.
6. Add the revelatory component	Start with words of knowledge for healing and prophesy over people.
7. Go with the flow and start evangelizing	Power comes first, then evangelism.
8. Keep adding risk	Prophesy and pray for groups of people. Make bolder claims of what Jesus will do.
9. Develop ministry teams	Introduce people to process and walk them through it. Training others is the best way for you to develop.
10. Develop teams	Develop teams that can prophesy, heal the sick and do evangelism together. Multiply what God has given you.

It is good to begin small, in a private group, instead of immediately trying to prophesy or heal the sick in large public service. Some people keep a detailed journal of what they have tried and what has or has not worked. How many words have I given? How many were accurate? How many people have

I prayed for healing? How many were healed? How many words of knowledge did I dare to give? How many were right?

Power Evangelism in Public

In a parable about a great banquet, Jesus talks about going to the streets to invite people to a celebration (see Luke 14:15-24). Let's just do that: let's go out and share the Gospel. Though daunting, practicing power evangelism with strangers is good. It is a great way to learn how to share God's love and power in a way that people can understand. The more you do it, the more you learn.

Whether you are at a restaurant or a grocery store, a divine encounter may be waiting for you. Jesus is our example in this. On his journey through Samaria, He rests at a public well by a town (see John 4). There, he meets a Samaritan woman shunned by her neighbors. This encounter leads to an entire town believing in Him.

In the Netherlands, I have discovered that certain groups of people are generally more open to having a "spiritual" conversation than others. If people are walking fast, clearly going somewhere in a hurry, they most likely will not be interested in stopping to have a conversation. If they are sitting around in a park or public place doing nothing, they may well be willing to talk.

I have also found that older people often have prejudices against Church and Jesus Christ, so they are not necessarily open for a conversation. I normally look for some young adults who are just hanging out so I can talk with them. Do not try to talk to everyone you see; instead, ask God to lead you to the right individuals. Some days, you may have a lot of conversations, other days few. It is like fishing; some days you have a lot of bites and other days you don't.

There are benefits to going to the same place every week to share the Gospel. Your role changes from that of a passing evangelist to that of a confidant. For three years, I have been going to the same people and the same place in Amsterdam every Tuesday night. The locals no longer see me as an evangelist, but as their pastor. They are looking forward to me coming. My going there every week shows people that I am not simply interested in preaching at them, but also listening and caring.

No matter how people react, do not give up. Julien Conor's testimony shows how perseverance wins the day.[36]

> After a crash course in power evangelism with Matt in Belgium, a spark was ignited inside me. Understanding something of how God could use me to prophesy and heal the sick, I wanted to share the power of this incredible love with everyone.
>
> Returning home to England after the week in Belgium, I was so stirred up to continue what God had started to do through me. I decided to go for a walk around town, meet people, heal the sick and prophesy. I was out for about an hour, and no one wanted to speak to me. I felt rejected. I stumbled over my words. I became so fearful to speak to anyone. In that next year, I only dared to give someone a prophetic word twice. I felt like a failure.

The next year, I went to a town called Cwmbran in Wales. There I experienced God move in a powerful way. I went with other believers to a skate park where roughly thirty young people were skating. I tried to begin a conversation by asking if I could test out their scooters. I have no experience with scooters, but thankfully I did not fall. I began speaking to them about Jesus and sharing the Gospel. Many listened, but not for very long. They kept one ear on what I was saying as they continued to skate. After I finished talking, I told them that Jesus is alive today and loves to show people how much He loves them. One way is through healing. Then I asked, "Do any of you have any pain?"

I guess being in a skate park, they all had a reason to raise their hands. I commanded one ankle to be healed in the name of Jesus and the young boy was healed instantly. He and his friends very surprised at the healing. (I was also a little surprised.)

They all wanted Jesus to heal them also, and He did! Around ten young people—everyone I prayed for—were healed. They all experienced God's power. At the end, I asked if the wanted to accept Jesus into their lives as Lord and Savior, and eight of them prayed to accept Jesus.

In the last three years, God has stretched me, and I have grown in power evangelism. I am amazed each time when Jesus heals someone or speaks into someone's life through me.

What I've Learned

Evangelism, like prophecy, is simple. Your job is not to argue with people, but to show them God's love and power in order to share the Gospel. The more you do it, the better you get at it.

To help you get going, I will share some steps you might take. However, I don't mean to turn power evangelism into a formula. Do not rely on the steps, keep listening to what the Holy Spirit is telling you to do. Experiment with the different suggestions and methods and figure out which works best for you.

Connect with God and with people – When approaching people there are many methods you can use to break the ice. Some people use a questionnaire about friendship to get a conversation started. I sometimes offer people a card with an encouraging text (scripture cards) to get talking. In his book *Conspiracy of Kindness*, Steve Sjogren shares a list of more than one hundred ways you can serve your community in order to share the gospel. His favorite was going to businesses to offer to clean their toilets for free. One AP Press article dubbed him the world record holder in voluntary toilet cleaning.[37]

The Vineyard Church in Amsterdam discovered one of their most effective evangelistic events was a three-day silent retreat with spiritual directors. The Holy Spirit Himself did His work in the lives of the participants.[38] The Holy Spirit is the greatest evangelist and He is the one who convicts people of sin and causes change in their lives. Our job as power evangelists is simply to do and say what we experience He is saying or doing.

Once I was in a Chilean megachurch with my father. I was about to speak, and asked my father about the right protocol there. He looked at me and said, "Just do what God tells you to do." Those words took off all the pressure I felt to act correctly and say the right things. At another event, a Holy Spirit weekend in Cyprus, I remember worrying about whether or not I would say and do the right things. Then I remembered Luke 12:11-12, where Jesus says that when we come before leaders, we should not worry about what to say. The Holy Spirit will teach us "what [we] ought to say."

Since that moment, preaching has become significantly easier for me. I am less concerned now with saying the "right" things and just try to listen to what the Holy Spirit is saying to me. In the same way, there is not one single right way to share the gospel. Just love God, love people and do what you feel God is leading you to do. You may be seriously surprised what God will do through you!

Whether you build a bridge with people by serving them or helping them first or simply start talking about God immediately, it is important that this is done with sensitivity and courage. There are many ways that you can connect with people and start a conversation. Sometimes I will open a conversation asking people whether I can give them a gift, like an encouraging word or a healing. If they are open to receiving prayer or an encouraging word, I pray for them or share what I see in them. I often share a word of knowledge. Generally, it is spot on, but at times, people say none of it is true. I also ask them if they have pain anywhere in their body. If they have pain, I pray for healing. The conversation is definitely easier if and when a healing takes place, but even if that does or does not happen, continue the conversation if the person is listening.

If you are praying for healing, pray quickly, as that may afford you more opportunities to pray again for healing. Remember, it is not the length of your prayer that heals people.

Share your testimony – Listen to people. Find out where they are regarding their beliefs and their faith in Christ. If appropriate, share your testimony of what Jesus has done in your life. Practice sharing your testimony succinctly. Tell how your life was before Christ, when you chose to follow Christ and what happened after you began your life with Christ.

If possible, present the Gospel – There are many different ways to give a Gospel presentation. I always try to have one ready I can give within one to two minutes. Often I will ask the person, "Can I give you a quick summary of the message of Jesus?" If they say yes, I share something like this:

> I believe in a spiritual source of perfect love, life and peace available for everyone. I call this source "God." Many people have misused the name of God for selfish and even unjust reasons, but that doesn't change who God really is. I still believe and experience His life today. I believe everyone consciously or unconsciously desires to know Him. I don't see God as an angry old man with a stick on a throne. I know God through Jesus. In Jesus, I see a radical message of love and acceptance for all who believe.

Jesus came not to condemn the world, but to save the world from our selfishness, fear and greed. Due to these things, we as humans are destroying each other, the environment and our world. This brokenness is what the Bible calls sin; something we all are affected by (Rom. 3:23). When we are left to our own devices, we create pain and separation from God and from each other (Rom. 6:23; 5:12). This pain and destruction is a downward spiral (2 Thess. 1:8-9).

Yet God does not want anyone to perish, so He sent Jesus to become our solution to our problems. Jesus came to earth and healed the sick, raised the dead and taught radical things that are totally opposite to the way many rulers of this world live. He never committed any crime or did anything wrong, yet willingly gave his life for us on the cross to take all of our hurt, sin and brokenness (2 Cor. 5:21).

He did not stay dead, though. After three days, He came back to life. He conquered the power of death—we no longer have to fear it. He wants everyone to be able to live free from anxiety, worry, depression and addiction. One of the reasons many people struggle with these issues is that they feel the pain of rejection, insecurity and are not sure if they can really be safe or belong.

Christ said that everyone who is burdened and tired can come to Him and receive true peace and rest (Matt. 11:28-30). Everyone in the world is actually searching for this. They are looking for something that can give them a security and peace of mind that is greater than their bank account, success or education.

Through Jesus Christ, the Bible says that we can come to know God as our Father. He is closer than the air we breathe and He can fill our hearts

HOW TO GROW IN POWER EVANGELISM

with a love and security that is indestructible. Can I share with you how you can experience and receive that reality today?

The first thing God asks for us is to turn to Him. The word "repentance" simply means to turn from whatever is keeping us from knowing God and walking toward him. It is saying, "God, I want to turn from everything that keeps me from You and from becoming the person You created me to be." The second step is to not just go to Him, but give Him your life. Jesus said that when we only live for ourselves, our own selfishness and ego, we are in danger of losing our lives. Yet when we give Him our lives, He gives us a new heart and a new way of looking at the world. Some describe this as being born again.

Let me ask you, if Jesus were here right now (which I believe He is), what would you say to Him if He said, "(Fill in person's name), I want you to know Me. I want to have a relationship with you. I want to take your hurt, pain, insecurity and sin upon Me." What would you say to Him? (Then be silent and wait for their response.)

If their response is that they would like to say yes to having a relationship with Jesus, ask them if they would like to pray with you right then. If you lead them in a prayer, allow them to welcome Jesus into their lives and confess anything they want to confess that may be in the way of them getting to know Him. (They don't have to confess their sins out loud.)

When appropriate, I use Romans 10:9-10, which speaks about confessing with our mouth that Jesus is Lord and believing that God raised him from the dead. Sometimes, I don't lead people in a prayer, but have them talk to Jesus for themselves and experience what He might answer them. Many times, I have seen people deeply touched by God when they begin asking Him questions and listening. My goal is not to get them pray a certain prayer, but to experience God's love and bring them closer to Jesus.

In the Red-Light District, for example, at times I ask people whether they want to experience God. If they say yes, I have them ask God short questions and be silent to see what they may hear or experience. Often, people experience God's "gentle whisper" (1 Kings 19:12, NLT), a heat, or a very deep significant peace. When people ask the Holy Spirit to do something (speak to them or touch them), quite often, He does. Our difficulty is that we don't have the patience or the faith to actually take the time to talk to and listen to the Holy Spirit.

The Holy Spirit is the best power evangelist ever. When you work together with Him and when people connect to Him directly, anything can happen.

At the end of a conversation, you may ask a question, like:

- Can I pray for you?
- Would it be okay if I bless you?
- Is there anything that you need prayer for?

The Next Step

When the people at the day of Pentecost asked Peter what they had to do to be saved, he responded by saying, "Repent and be baptized every one of you in the name of Jesus Christ for the forgiveness of your sins, and you will receive the gift of the Holy Spirit" (Acts 2:38).

This means that repenting or turning our lives toward God and away from sin should be followed up by baptism in water and baptism in the Holy Spirit.

Paul describes baptism in water as this:

> Do you not know that all of us who have been baptized into Christ Jesus were baptized into his death? We were buried therefore with him by baptism into death, in order that, just as Christ was raised from the dead by the glory of the Father, we too might walk in newness of life.
> – ROMANS 6:3-4

Water baptism is not only an integral part of the great commission, but it is an illustration of what a life with Christ is all about (Matt. 28:18-20). Our old identity is dead (crucified and buried) through Christ's death and we arise from the water with the new resurrection life of Christ in us. In Christ, we are new creations and we have his life and power available to guide us (2 Cor. 5:17).

There is also another empowerment available to all believers called the infilling or the baptism of the Holy Spirit. In the book of Acts, when people were filled with the Holy Spirit they often spoke in new tongues (Acts 2:1-4; 8:14-17; 10:44-46), received healing (9:15-19) or began speaking in tongues and prophesying (19:1-7). Such experiences are still available to all believers and often prove to be life-changing. We should not be content to only be filled once. In Ephesians 5:18, the Greek verb translated as to "be filled with" the Holy Spirit can be translated as "continually be filled with" the Holy Spirit. We should continually grow in His fruit and in His gifts (Gal. 5:22-23; 1 Cor. 14:5-11).

All of this is done in the context of a spiritual family called the Church. I am not speaking about the Church as an organization first, but as a body. A body where Christ is the head and all of us believers make up distinct but diverse parts. One is the hand, the other the foot and yet another the eye (see 1 Cor. 12:14-18). It is in this family that we learn to live our lives with the Gospel at the core of our identity. We learn what it is to honor Christ in every part of our lives.

We also learn how to forgive, deal with conflict and love each other as Christ loves us. As anything made up of humans, we are imperfect and we do not always have the best track record of being "Christ-like." If I were God, I would have chosen another vehicle for bringing my message to the world! Fortunately, I am not. He has given us, His Church, the mission of bringing His presence to the world by obeying Him and sharing His love and words wherever we go. You just never know how giving someone a cup of coffee and a word from the Lord can change their lives forever. Just listen to Riley's story.

Is Your Name Riley?

Riley had been struggling with a deep depression. One night, in his hotel room, he started saying out loud, "There is no hope for my life. There is no purpose for my life and no reason to go on living."

The next morning, a man walked up to him and put a cup of coffee in his hand and said, "Is your name Riley?"

"Yes, it is," responded Riley.

The stranger said, "God spoke to me last night about you."

Riley scoffed, "That's nice. He speaks to you, buddy, but He does not speak to me."

The man then replied, "He told me to come and tell you that your life does have hope and because you are alive there is a purpose for it."

Just a few hours after Riley's desperate words in his hotel room, God sent someone to turn all that around.

Then, Riley walked back to his hotel and on his way, a woman asked him, "Excuse me, are you a Christian?"

Riley meant to say no, but found himself saying, "Yes."

This lady was just asking for directions to a local church. He gave her instructions and continued on his way. But something had shifted in his heart when he answered the question by saying yes.

By the time he got back to his room, he was shaking. He got down on his knees and then had a vision where he was under a building that had collapsed. God asked him, "Can you lift the burden that is on your life?"

Riley cried out, "No."

God responded, "It is already done. Just move forward and don't look back."

In the vision, the rubble that had been on top of him had disappeared. He was free. He felt the heavy pressure removed from his chest. He could breathe again. God had lifted the heaviness off of him. He was now able to turn away from his old way of life.

Riley is now a pastor in Perth, Australia.[39]

CONCLUSION

Just Do "The Stuff"

> You mean I gave up drugs for *that?*
> – JOHN WIMBER

> The seeds that fell among the thorns represent those who hear the message, but all too quickly the message is crowded out by the cares and riches and pleasures of this life. And so they never grow into maturity.
> – LUKE 8:14 (NLT)

What is your dream? What is your passion? Do you want to prophesy, heal the sick, get words of knowledge and lead people to Jesus? Do you want to grow in power evangelism? What steps are you taking to make that a reality?

Often we are over-taught and under-challenged to do what God has inspired us to do. Let me challenge you now. Are you going to put this book on the shelf and forget what you have just read, or are you going to do something about it?

My friend Juriaan Beek has seen many people get healed on the streets of the Netherlands. His strategy of cultivating and developing this ministry was very simple. He decided that every week, he was going to go out and pray for people. He would not worry about whether they were going to be healed or not. The more he stepped out, the more healings and miracles took place. One of the experiences that really helped change his life was when he saw a paralyzed woman healed while he was ministering at a psychic fair.[40] That's what experiencing the power of God does.

Many times, when I pray for the sick or give words of encouragement on the streets, people think I am crazy. Yet I have seen people's lives changed by taking radical steps of faith. If my fear of people's "no" paralyzes me, I will not get to experience the healings, signs and wonders that might take place when people say yes. When you say yes, anything is possible.

> It is not because things are difficult that we do not dare, it is because we do not dare that things are difficult.
> – SENECA

Do "The Stuff"

In 1963, John Wimber was a "beer guzzling, drug abusing pop musician, who was converted at the age of 29 while chain-smoking his way through a Quaker-led Bible study."[41]

Wimber found the church services rather boring, but he was fascinated by Jesus' supernatural healings, signs and wonders. After going to the church for several weeks, he finally went to a church leader and asked, "When do we get to do the stuff?"

"What stuff?" the leader replied.

"You know, the stuff here in the book. The stuff Jesus did,

like healing the sick, raising the dead, healing the blind—stuff like that."

"Those sort of things don't happen anymore," the leader answered.

"You mean I gave up drugs for *that*?" Wimber replied incredulously.[42]

Wimber took the Gospels to be true. What Jesus said and taught should be *done* (see Luke 9:1-2; 10:1-3; Matt. 28:18-20). He was not content to only have an intellectual faith, but desired to experience God's love and power as well. I agree.

Don't Get Too Comfortable

So what's stopping you from doing the stuff? A dangerous addiction for Bible-believing Christians is living for comfort and for the approval of others. Comfort and fear of people can choke out a dynamic faith. An ancient folk tale shows how that might work.

> There once was a man I will call Harry. He had received a special gift from the gods: a little nutshell with a red cord hanging out of it that had very special powers. Whenever Harry had a problem, all he had to do was pull the red cord and the problem would be over. For example, if he had a test on Friday, he would pull the red cord on Thursday and it would be Saturday. He had passed the test. Harry was so happy with his shell and the little red cord that he always kept it with him.
>
> A difficult discussion with his boss, wife, or kids was always solved by pulling on the little red cord. This little red cord was his secret to success

and happiness. With it, he was able to achieve the Western dream of owning a house, two cars, 2.5 kids and a dog.

Harry felt he had everything under control. Harry loved his feeling of safety. He liked seeing his kids grow up and succeed in school. When his children had relational problems or when they needed him to be around, he would pull on the cord and everything would be solved. What an ideal life ... right?

Wrong!

Harry never experienced seeing his children's birth or wondering if he could make a mortgage payment because the little red cord took care of all his fears and discomfort. He never worked to get close to people because he had a safe solution for everything. He had become a slave to being comfortable.

When Harry turned ninety, his wife passed away. He looked back and realized he had never really *lived*. Because he had always chosen the "safe" route, he had never experienced real pain, difficulty, joy, peace, or the delight of a great victory. Now that his life was nearly over, all he had was regrets. What a tragedy.

Taking risks means that I refuse to be a slave to *comfort*. I will not pull on the red cord and avoid difficulties and problems. We only get to live life once. There is no dress rehearsal.

Do you dare to throw away the red cord in your life and start living today? What is keeping you from turning off the "safe mode" of life and doing what you were made for?

Receiving and Passing On

In 2010, after spending some time with a prophet in Chicago. I asked him how I could prophesy, and he responded, "The same Holy Spirit I have, you do too. Just do it!"

In that same year, after reading books by John Wimber and Gary Best from the Vineyard movement, similar kinds of miracles and healings began taking place in my life as the ones that I read about. Phil Strout, the current leader of that movement, also laid his hands on me and blessed me. That year, my prophetic and healing ministry grew exponentially. What these people imparted to me, I want to pass along to others. I have written this book so that what has happened in my life can also develop in yours.

Just read what happened in the life of the person who sent me this testimony on Facebook.

> Hey Matt! You don't know this, but you've had a really big impact on me – especially in prophesying and healing the sick. It was about two or three years ago when we met. The lessons you taught and the words God spoke into my life through you have really helped me to grow in the area of spiritual gifts and reaching out to the lost. I have seen so many people touched by the love of God through a healing or a word of knowledge. All glory to God who gives to all freely!

I want to see you, the person reading this book, equipped and released to prophesy, get words of knowledge and heal the sick.

Do you want to do the same kind of things Jesus did? Is Jesus Christ the Lord and Savior of every area of your life? Do you want to live a Christianity that is not just about talk, but of power (see 1 Cor. 4:20)?

If so, then let your faith be greater than your fear. Allow God's Spirit to fill your heart with His love so that you can love others in the same way that He loves us. Then step out by faith. The same Holy Spirit I have, you have too! Just do it!

> Heal the sick, raise the dead, cleanse lepers, cast out demons. You received without paying; give without pay.
> — MATTHEW 10:8

Notes

1. Wimber, J., *Power Evangelism* (Grand Rapids, MI: Chosen Books, 1986).
2. Putman, P., *School of Kingdom Ministry* (Oklahoma, OK: Coaching Saints Publications, 2018), 162.
3. PAZ International is a church-planting movement started in the Amazon basin of Brazil. The mother church in Santarem has more than 50,000 members. They currently have churches in Japan, Italy, Portugal, Venezuela and Cape Verde. See www.projectamazon.org (accessed January 14th 2020).
4. God's emotions toward us form an ongoing theme in Mike Bickle's teachings. An example of a sermon where he talks about this is *Living with the Assurance that God Enjoys Us*. See www.ihopkc.org (accessed 31 October 31st 2019).
5. Rolheiser, R., *Prayer: Our Deepest Longing* (Cincinnati, OH: Franciscan Media, 2013).
6. Cooke, G., *Approaching the Heart of Prophecy* (Vacaville, CA: Brilliant Book House, 2006), 38.
7. Marilyn Manson is a controversial heavy metal musician whose autobiography and early music regularly quote satanist Aleister Crowley. One of his albums is titled *Antichrist Superstar*.
8. McGerr, P., "Johnny Lingo's Eight Cow Wife." Published in James Dobson, *Night Light* (Colorado Springs, CO: Multnomah, 2000), 196.
9. Willard, D., *Renovation of the Heart* (Carol Stream, IL: NavPress 2012), Chapter 6.
10. Not her real name.
11. Keller, T., *Deconstructing Defeater Beliefs*. Found on www.welcometoredeemer.com/resources/articles (accessed October 9th 2019).
12. This the same scale as the Engle Scale of Evangelism except it has an extra dimension of telling whether people are open or closed.
13. Research by the Dutch Central Bureau of Statistics, CBS. Source: https: nos.nl/artikel/2233860-we-vertrouwen-de-politie-het-meest-en-de-kerk-het-minst.html (accessed October 28th 2019).
14. In his book *The Reason for God* (New York, NY: Penguin, 2009), Timothy Keller counters seven common defeater beliefs: 1) There can't be only *one* true religion. 2) How could a good God allow suffering? 3) Christianity is a straitjacket. 4) The Church is responsible for so much injustice. 5) How can a loving God send people to hell? 6) Science has disproved Christianity. 7) You can't take the Bible literally.
15. Cole, N., *Cultivating a Life for God* (Long Beach, CA: CMA, 2012), 108.
16. Gonzales J. E., *Secrets of the Healing Ministry* (Scotts Valley, CA: CreateSpace, 2015), 37-41.
17. Some of Nouwen's sermons about this can be found on YouTube, *Being the Beloved*.
18. Cooke, *Approaching the Heart of Prophecy*, 107.
19. Willard, D., *The Divine Conspiracy* (San Francisco, CA: Harper, 1997), 22, 25.

20. The video of Marije de Vries' healing can be found on YouTube, titled *Jesus Heals Today*, add: Matthew Helland. It is in Dutch with subtitles. Accessed December 10th, 2019.
21. Wimber, *Power Evangelism*, 42-44.
22. Todd White's testimony can be found on YouTube, search for "Todd White Healing Testimony."
23. Seng, J., *Miracle Work: A Down-to-Earth Guide to Supernatural Ministries* (Downers Grove, IL: IVP, 2013), 240.
24. Marlene Klepees' dramatized testimony can be found on YouTube, *Woman Healed of Cerebral Palsy Through Vision*. Accessed November 25th, 2019.
25. Wimber, *Power Evangelism*, 2008, 173.
26. David Betts, Amsterdam 2010 New Wine Conference.
27. Cooke, *Approaching the Heart of Prophecy*, 48.
28. Putman, P., *School of Kingdom Ministry Prayer Model Cards*. Available at schoolofkingdomministry.org (accessed January 11th 2019).
29. This section draws heavily on David Betts' teaching at the 2010 New Wine Conference in Amsterdam.
30. Cooke, *Approaching the Heart of Prophecy*, 33-35.
31. My father, Dean Helland, sent me this story in a personal email on April 10th 2016.
32. Bolz, S., *Translating God*. (Glendale, CA: ICreate Productions, 2015), 162. On YouTube, Shawn Bolz shares a video about getting words of knowledge wrong. You will find it under the title *You're Either Right or Wrong. Teaching Moment*. Accessed on January 21st, 2020.
33. www.charismamag.com, type key words "Osborn taught evangelist Daniel King" (accessed December 12th 2019).
34. Based on Putman, *School of Kingdom Ministry*, 177.
35. See www.prophesyandheal.com for my online school of prophesy levels 1 and 2 (accessed 14th January 2020).
36. Julien Conor personally shared this testimony with me.
37. www.stevesjogren.com/cleaning-toilets/ (accessed November 1st 2019). Steve Sjogren, *Conspiracy of Kindness* (Bloomington, MN: Bethany House, 2008).
38. Pickerell, E., *The Secular Mystic: Mysticism and the Future of Faith in the West* (Master's Thesis from Vrije Universiteit in Amsterdam, August 2013), 112-113.
39. Riley (not his real name) told me his testimony through a recording on WhatsApp around August 1st 2019.
40. See this healing on YouTube, titled *Amhem: genezing verlamde vrouw*. It is in Dutch, without subtitles. Accessed November 25th, 2019.
41. Pickerell, *The Secular Mystic*, 78.
42. *Ibid,* 78

Recommended Resources

PROPHECY
Bickle, M., *Growing in the Prophetic* (Lake Mary, FL: Charisma, 2008)
Bolz, S., *Translating God* (Glendale, CA: ICreate Productions, 2015)
Cooke, G., *Approaching the Heart of Prophecy* (Vacaville, CA: Brilliant Book House, 2006)
Eckhardt, J., *The Prophet's Manual* (Lake Mary, FL: Charisma, 2017)
Goll, Jim W., *The Seer* (Shippensburg, PA: Destiny Image, 2004)
Hagin, K., *How You Can Be Led by the Spirit of God* (Broken Arrow, OK: Faith Library Publications, 2006)
Helland, M., *Prophesy—Just Do It!* (Haarlem, NL: Arrowz, 2019)
Willard, D., *Hearing God: Developing a Conversational Relationship with God* (Downers Grove, IL: IVP, 2012)

HEALING
Clark, R., *Authority to Heal* (Grand Rapids, MI: Baker, 2016)
Clark, R., *The Healing Breakthrough* (Grand Rapids, MI: Baker, 2016)
Dawkins, R., *Do What Jesus Did* (Grand Rapids, MI: Chosen Books, 2013)
Roberts, O., *Expect a Miracle* (Nashville, TN: Thomas Nelson, 1995)
Wimber, J., *Power Healing* (New York, NY: HarperOne, 2009)

SPIRITUAL GIFTS
Bijl, J., *Activating Your Spiritual Gifts* (Scotts Valley, CA: CreateSpace, 2016)
Best, G., *Naturally Supernatural: God May Be Closer Than You Think.* (Cape Town: Vineyard International Publishing, 2008)
Putman, P., *Kingdom Impact* (Grand Rapids, MI: Chosen Books, 2019)
Putman, P., *School of Kingdom Ministry* (Oklahoma, OK: Coaching Saints Publications, 2013
Wimber, J., *Everyone Gets to Play* (Boise, ID: Ampelon Publishing, 2009)

CHURCH & CHURCH PLANTING
Cole, N., *Organic Church* (San Francisco, CA: Jossey-Bass, 2009)
Cole, N., *Cultivating a Life for God* (Long Beach, CA: CMA Resource, 2012)
Keller, T., *Center Church: Doing Balanced, Gospel-Centered Ministry in Your City* (Grand Rapids, MI: Zondervan, 2012)
Keller, T., *Redeemer Church Planting Manual* (New York, NY: Redeemer City to City, 2002)
Dynamic Church Planting International www.dcpi.org (a practical three day training on how to plant a church in your context.)

THE GOSPEL
Keller, T., *The Prodigal God* (New York, NY: Penguin, 2011)
Keller, T., *The Reason for God* (New York, NY: Penguin, 2009)
Putman, P., *Live Like Jesus* (Grand Rapids, MI: Chosen Books, 2017)
Willard, D., *Renovation of the Heart* (Carol Stream, IL: NavPress 2012)
Willard, D., *The Divine Conspiracy* (San Francisco, CA: Harper, 1997)

(POWER) EVANGELISM
Accad, F. E., *Building Bridges: Christianity and Islam* (Carol Stream, IL: NavPress, 1997)
Coleman, R. E., *The Master Plan of Evangelism* (Grand Rapids, MI: Revell, 2010)
Dedmon, K., *The Ultimate Treasure Hunt* (Shippensberg, PA: Destiny Image, 2007)
King, P., *Light Belongs in the Darkness* (Shippensburg, PA: Destiny Image Publishers, 2005)
Seng, J., *Miracle Work* (Downers Grove, IL: IVP, 2013)
Sjogren, S., *Conspiracy of Kindness* (Bloomington, MN: Bethany House, 2008)
Stibbe, M., *Prophetic Evangelism* (Milton Keynes, UK: Authentic Media, 2004)

Matthew Helland

Born in Chile to American missionaries, Matthew Helland is an international missionary, speaker and writer. He is based out of Amsterdam, the Netherlands. In the past few years his ministry has taken him to nations throughout Europe, North America, South America, the Middle East and to Australia. He is fluent in English, Dutch and Spanish.

Matthew's first book with Arrowz publishing house was *Prophesy—Just Do It!* He feels called to activate churches in evangelism and the gifts of the Spirit. He frequently teaches on subjects such as:

- discipleship
- prophecy
- power evangelism
- divine healing
- prayer
- church planting
- radical generosity

Matthew and his wife, Femke, live in Amsterdam with their four children. After planting a church there, they are now focusing on reaching out to Spanish-speaking individuals in the city's Red-Light District. There, they are seeing lives transformed by the love of God and the power of the Holy Spirit.

www.newlifeequip.org
www.facebook.com/mattandfemke.helland

IMPACT
Prophesy and Change the World

Prophecy transforms people's lives, but it is meant for more. God is ready to transform every segment of society, and He reveals strategies to accomplish it.

Arleen Westerhof shows us how to work with prophetic revelation. She describes how to give prophetic words, test prophecies, and how apostles and prophets can work together to accomplish breakthrough. She shows that character development, inner healing and deliverance are essential for anyone building a prophetic ministry.

This practical book proves that prophecy can have an amazing impact on every aspect of the world around us!

TRADE PAPERBACK
192 PAGES
8.5 X 5.4 X 0.4 IN
ISBN ITP: 9781951014018
ISBN EBOOK: 9781951014025
RRP $15.99

DR. ARLEEN WESTERHOF is the founder and director of the Netherlands Prophetic Council. She initiated the Living in Your Destiny Schools of the Prophets and founded Women on the Frontlines in the Netherlands. Arleen regularly speaks at conferences all over the world. Together with her husband Dick, she leads God's Embassy Amsterdam, a church and apostolic center. Her passion is using prophecy to equip people to bring transformation to the different areas of society.

PROPHESY JUST DO IT!

You Can Prophesy

Would you be willing to prophesy if it were God's will for you to do so? It is His will! The Bible says, "You can all prophesy one by one, so that all may learn and all be encouraged" (1 Cor. 14:31).

MATTHEW HELLAND

Discover how you can nurture and develop your ability to hear God's voice and prophesy. With more than thirty practical exercises, you can learn (individually or in a group) how to distinguish God's voice and how to prophesy well. Be encouraged by the testimonies and anecdotes that demonstrate the power of prophecy. Don't hold back. *Prophesy—Just Do It!*

POWERPOCKET
144 PAGES
4.7 X 0.4 X 6.7 IN
ISBN PP: 9789490489526
ISBN EBOOK: 9781951014032
RRP $12.99

MATTHEW HELLAND (M.Div., Oral Roberts University) has led schools of prophecy around the world since 2010. Together with his wife, Femke, he works as a pastor in Amsterdam's Red-Light District. Matt and Femke have four children.

www.ingramcontent.com/pod-product-compliance
Lightning Source LLC
Chambersburg PA
CBHW030153100526
44592CB00009B/252